Normz
Waiheke
stories

Normz
Waiheke
Stories

Lynne Beatty (18), Norm Stephens (23)
Beatty House, New Lynn
November 1959

Norm Stephens

Press

Published by 99% Press,
an imprint of Lasavia Publishing Ltd.
Auckland, New Zealand
www.lasaviapublishing.com

Copyright © Norm Stephens, 2022
Editor: Rowan Sylva
Design: Daniela Gast

ISBN: 978-1-99-116058-4

To my grandchildren:

Samuel, Emily, Jackson and Leliana

Foreword

I first met Norm and Lynne when they moved into the Waiheke Retirement Village in 2015. When I asked keen story teller and writer, Norm Stephens, to provide a piece or two for the monthly village newsletter, little did I know that his stories and tales, written in longhand, would evoke such memories of people and places of my own upbringing in Ostend in the fifties till I first left the island in the early seventies. Many of the people mentioned were known to me and my family. My older brothers and sisters attended school in Onetangi. I attended school in Ostend and we all went to the Onetangi Hotel. The opportunity to read about my old stomping grounds through the eyes and life experiences of another was not to be missed. This has been a heart-warming, familiar, funny, sometimes sad, but always entertaining trip down memory lane. Thanks for sharing, Norm. It's been priceless.

Libby Kruis, Waiheke Retirement Village Manager, Waiheke 2022

Contents

Acknowledgements

Thanks to Waiheke Retirement Village manager, Libby Kruis, for asking me to write some short stories for her Village Bulletin. This got me back into writing mode, a few stories grew too. In early December 2021 I handed my final copy to Libby, a week later I was away again with another four, then another two in the New Year. That's it or I'll go on forever. Thanks to Libby for her encouragement and patience when turning my handwritten copies into typewritten copies. My writing I know, is getting uneven due to macular degeneration.

Thanks to Lynne, my loving wife, travel companion, and now full-time carer, for listening to my ideas and drafts. Thanks to my greater family of eleven, with one on the way, and dog, Max, for listening to my jokes and stories. Thanks to the village residents who read my stories and listened to my jokes and yarns at Christmas lunches. Thanks also for their encouragements and their comments. These stories also reminded them of their experiences. Several were reminded of their own days, staying in the old type baches with no power, cooking on primus or wood stoves, lighting kerosene lamps to read, playing games and sleeping in bunks and sleeping bags.

Thanks to Waiheke author Mike Johnson for his help and advice. A big thanks also to Rowan and Daniela who have worked hard as editors layouters and designers to get this book out. I would also like to thank the doctors, nurses, and other staff at the Ostend Medical Centre and Waiheke Health Trust for their valuable assistance to both Lynne and I. Thanks also to St. Johns Ambulance and the rescue helicopter. Waiheke is lucky to have such valuable people. I have enjoyed writing these stories and the memories they have rekindled.

Love to you all,
Norm

Introduction

Throughout my schooldays, I usually ranked in the top ten in the English exams at Seddon Tech. I was third both years I was there. I was also third in maths. My only other scholastic achievement was top of the class in standard-two history. My teacher at Point Chevalier Primary School, standard-four, was a Miss Paterson who was to have a huge influence in my future. She deeply embarrassed me when criticizing my writing by making me name the best writer in class. After looking at everyone's efforts, the winner was obviously one of the girls. That made me blush, but my writing made a major improvement.

Miss Paterson encouraged me to read more books, not to rely on a dictionary, and to have confidence in my spelling. I think she would be pleased to see my pride and joy: a floor to ceiling bookshelf containing over four hundred books, mostly rugby league, other sport, NZ murders, and war books, but also, my favourite authors, Barry Crump, Alan Duff and James Hadley Chase.

Over the years, especially when Lynne and I travelled, I've written diaries. After our big 1986 OE, I wrote an article for the NZ Herald. I have also written for boxing and rugby league magazines. When I turned fifty, I took on the recommendation of learning a new skill each year until I retired at sixty. The first year was home brewing beer (since stopped for health reasons), then nurturing plants and seedlings. The third year was writing short stories. I didn't get to the fourth year as government of the day changed the retirement age to sixty-five.

I entered several writing competitions and came third in my first effort. I then won the 1994 Waiheke Writers Group competition with my story 'Flounder Flats' (included in this volume). In 1996 I wrote a novel, 'Snow,' a fiction based on fact, a story of the Waiheke walkabouts and adventures of Snow and Artie (Lynne's uncle

Eddie and myself) I tried to get it published but was unsuccessful. When New Zealand went into lockdown in August 2021, Waiheke Retirement Village manager, Libby Kruis, asked me for a couple of my short stories to reprint for her village monthly bulletin. At Lynne's suggestion I decided to write about my experiences on the island. From a few stories it grew as more topics came to mind. Even after three months of writing and informing Libby that I had finished, more recollection came to my memory, more stories evolved. I hope that those who read my efforts will enjoy them. Maybe they even bring some old memories back to reflect on.

These stories are not meant to be a history of Waiheke Island, nor written in chronological order. They are seen through my eyes from when I first visited the island as a ten-year-old to the present time, seventy-five years later. Some readers may see them in a different perspective. That is their prerogative.

Norm Stephens, Waihke Island 17/12/2021

Part 1

Norm's First Waiheke Holiday

My first big Christmas holiday was to Ostend on Waiheke Island. Funnily enough Ostend is now my 'Home'. It was around 1946. I was ten. My family and Mum's sister hired the back area of the holiday accommodation on the corner of Ostend Road and Wharf Road (the one with the recently built swimming pool).

What an adventure it was and seventy-five years later it's still one of my best memories. We boarded *the Baroona* at King's Wharf, and sailed across the gulf with dolphins diving around the boat's bow leading us into Putiki Bay. I remember seeing the two farmhouses on the right-hand side (still there) and the homestead on the left, now owned by the Goldwater family. For many years in later life, arriving in the bay made me feel I was coming home.

After landing at Ostend Wharf, we walked, lugging our bags to the boarding-house-style accommodation. We had the back three rooms containing two bedrooms and a dining room/kitchen. Mum, Dad, and younger sister, Marion, shared one bedroom and Aunty Grace and Uncle Tom the other. My cousins, Terry (the oldest by two years) and David (same age as me), and I slept in a corrugated iron shed with a wooden floor about ten feet by ten feet with a double mattress on the ground. Behind us, on the Ostend Road side, was the Ostend Hall where several dances were held during our visit. We three boys used to sit up and sing along with the music (yes, remember when you could actually know what they were singing about). The entrance area to the hall is still standing, but the hall area has gone.

At the back of the building there was a shop at ground level that sold soft drinks, ice cream, lollies and penny gobstoppers as big as a ping-pong ball. Up the road between Ladd Road and Albert Crescent was a general store, where it stands to this day, that sold all the supplies the 'oldies' needed – no supermarkets or takeaways. The intrepid sailor Johnny Wray sold fish at the Ostend Wharf and I caught my first fish there – a massive six-inch snapper. Cousin David threw his line in but forgot to tie the other end down. Everyday was a new adventure. We played cricket on the concrete pitch at the sports ground (the only building in those days was the toilet block for boaties), walked around the foreshore to Anzac Bay (never thought I'd return to live there). We walked to Palm Beach and once to Onetangi (the metal roads) for picnics. The motorbike tourist trophy races over two days provided great entertainment, but the highlight of the holiday was the Big Athletic and Axemen Day at the Woolshed on Onetangi Straight.

The Sports Day was an annual event and was in the farm paddock that is now the seventh-hole-fairway of the golf course. It was great for kids. The prize money was one shilling for a win, six pence for second, and three pence for third. My sister, even at six, was a good runner. I wasn't too bad at picnic meetings. I was quite fast off the mark and would start out wide to avoid the crowding in the middle. We won our races and combined in the three-legged and wheelbarrow events to win. I also won my sack races. We went home with a pocket full of 'bobs' plus tons of prickles in our feet, which Mum had to dig out with a needle. Alas all good things come to an end. After two glorious weeks it was time to go.

My older cousin Terry, a somewhat mischievous guy, had come up with a 'plan' to lock the double long drop toilets before we left. It was quite simple. The structure was built of old corrugated iron and the doorstops on the two doors were pieces of timber screwed onto the doorframe. It was just a matter of reaching through from one toilet area to the other and turning the doorstop to lock one, then tying a knot around the other door stop and threading the loose end of the string through one of the nail holes in the corrugated iron, then pushing the string back through the hole. Bingo – both doors locked. We can all imagine the next scenario. This was done moments before our walk back to Ostend Wharf and the ferry back home. As the next Christmas holidays were coming along the 'oldies' were dead keen to go back to Ostend. I was as scared as hell the owner would remember us, but thankfully Mum went along with going to Oneroa instead. The 'oldies' never found out about our (Terry's) prank.

First Holiday at Onetangi

My Aunty Grace, who lived in the Auckland neighbourhood of Three Kings, had neighbours, the Steele family, who had a bach on Victoria Road, Onetangi. Early in the New Year of 1950 they allowed her to have the bach for two weeks after they had used it over Christmas and New Year. My two cousins, Terry and David, myself, then aged thirteen, plus the Steeles' youngest son, Jimmy, also thirteen, headed to the island. We had two wonderful weeks at a beach I was destined to spend many years of my life at.

Everyone was up by 8am. We made our own bunks, then breakfast. A big chore was to replenish the firewood for the wood stove, as there was no electricity on the island in those days. There was, however, a plentiful supply of wood as several pine trees had been felled at the back of the long section. We used a two-man-crosscut-saw, handsaw and axe to cut logs and kindling to length. Aunty also used a Primus for cooking and light was provided by kerosene lamps. When cutting the wood and carrying it into the bach, we had to watch out for the biggest wetas I've ever seen. They were all over those logs.

After all the chores were completed, including morning dishes, it was off to the beach, sliding on nikau fronds down the track that went from Marine View Parade to Waiheke Road. We returned the fronds to the top on the way home. We would spend the day swimming, playing cricket at low tide, and exploring the rocks at the eastern end. Aunty would bring our lunch to the beach.

In the late afternoon we would fill a bucket with tuatuas dug out of the sand in the area in front of where the toilet and barbecue area is today. Aunty would make us what we termed pipi fritters. Us four boys would have a competition to see who could eat the most. Jimmy, a bigger lad than us was usually the winner. I've never eaten pipi fritters since – definitely not. I've eaten toheroas, white bait, and mussel fritters regularly - just no tuatuas.

Jimmy wore the same red boxer shorts every day. He also swam and slept in them. He lived in them for the whole two weeks. Jimmy loved to think he was the boss, but he wasn't the brightest. Elder cousin Terry would bait him something terrible. Terry would ask him sports questions, Jimmy would answer regardless of whether he knew the answer or not, Terry would then ask me the answer. Jimmy was often wrong. Then Terry would laugh at him, Jimmy's face going as red as his shorts.

After dinner, it was cards around the table with Terry constantly giving Jimmy a hard time. Kids will be kids. One day, for a change, we went down the back of the Steeles' section and on to the hill on the other side of Hobson Terrace. The hillside was in knee high grass. Lichtenstein & Arnoldson, a development company, had purchased several parcels of land in the Onetangi and Palm Beach areas, and had had them surveyed and pegged. Big bad cuzzie, Terry, had a bayonet, and his favourite trick was to slice the peg down the middle and throw it away. This rebounded on me seven years later when I purchased a section there, and yes, I had to search for pegs. Luckily all four pegs on the section I had selected were there.

We moved on up the road to where it made a sharp left-hand turn, now called Glow Worm Grove. A waterfall came down from between two big pumice-type rocks just below Trig Hill Road, running down and through a culvert under the road forming a large pool. Kids caught freshwater lobster there. We went up the right side of the waterfall (now gone dry) and Terry used his bayonet to cut down nikau fronds to build a hut. I was not to know that the section we were on, plus the next two, was owned by Joyce Beatty. Later the Beatty bach would be built there. The Beatties had four daughters, one of which was nine years old at the time. Later I would meet and marry her. Her name was Lynne.

Sadly, all good things come to an end, our wonderful two weeks were over, it was back to Point Chevalier and the thrill of the 1950's British Empire Games, the first big event I was to go to. I went to all four athletic days at Eden Park and the closing night, cycling at Western Springs Stadium. After that it was time for my first of two years at Seddon Tech in the city. Yet the memory of Onetangi never left me and gave me a burning desire to have my own bach there one day, or somewhere else as exotic. The dream was always there. I never really thought it would happen. But sometime dreams come true.

Footnote: Carol, the elder girl in the Steele family later married Jimmy Lockie, the bach became their home. Jimmy became the local electrician, he wired our baches as we moved, then renovated. Jimmy is nowadays our friendly neighbour at the village (WRV). Sadly, Carol passed away the first year we were here.

The Beatty Bach

I Left Seddon Tech at the end of my fourth form year at fifteen. I had taken a woodwork course, which was a bad move, as I was hopeless at woodwork practice. In fact, all my projects were so bad I wasn't allowed to take any home. At technical drawing and woodwork theory, I was reasonable. Science, I read a book at the back of the class. History was all about the Ming Dynasty and I wasn't interested. I should probably have gone to Mt. Albert Grammar, which by bike was closer than Seddon Tech in the city and taken an accountancy course. Sport at Seddon was great though, and I entered everything, anything to get a day away from the classroom.

The first time I met Lynne was on the eleventh of March 1956, her fifteenth birthday. The meeting was at the office of soft goods merchants Macky, Logan & Caldwell Ltd. Her uncle, Barry Smith had arranged the position of office clerk for her. I was nineteen at the time and Barry was my boss.

Macky's office was on the fifth floor of a wooden building that bordered Victoria, Elliot, and Darby Streets. It would've been a bloody nightmare if it ever caught fire like Auckland's John Burns and Christchurch's Ballantines. The office was like something out of a Charles Dickens' novel. The desks were old-style with shelves and pigeonholes in front and a long board across the top, drawers on both sides plus hooks to hang clipboards. I loved it, somewhere for everything.

The phones were similar to what you saw in gangster movies, Macky's were probably the only outfit that still had them. They had a separate piece held in one hand to the ear, the other hand was on a lamp shade type stand with a mouthpiece you spoke into. The girls would usually bend over to answer with one elbow on the desk. It was the days when women wore tight dresses, and they were an easy target for my accurate-aimed demon-flicking of rubber bands. It all came to an end one day when the accountant, wearing leather soled shoes slipped on a rubber band on the wooden floor and went into a rather ungainly skid. He stopped, stared straight at me, and in a loud commanding voice said, 'The next person I see flicking a rubber band will be fired on the spot.' That was the end of that.

Another naughty trick I was guilty of, was one involving a rubber mouse on a long length of thin white string. I would go up to the sixth floor where the lunchroom was situated, place the mouse in the passageway floor leading to the lunchroom. I would hide behind some boxes waiting to hear the rattly old lift come up. Then I would hear the sound of the old metal doors banging open, and the person would step out, turn left, make three steps, and then turn left again. It was easy to know if it was a man or a woman approaching as the women's high heels made a louder noise. I counted three steps, pause, one-step, pause, and then pull the string. The men usually laughed but the woman screamed. That sent me into laughter. After a few days I was advised to stop or there would be a compliant to management. I complied. These days, no doubt, such antics would be considered sexual harassment.

I guess, I was like many older teenagers of the day. I completed my compulsory military training, had my own '37 Morris 8 car, went to work in suit and tie, played footie, drank beer, and went to parties and dances. It was the start of the rock-n-roll era and I felt bullet proof. My fellow brother in arms, Graeme Ross, later became my brother-in-law. After dinner on Saturday nights, we would have a couple of beers, then off to the Point Chevalier Sailing Club. We would spot two girls together, have several dances with them, offer to take them home and often arrange to go to the Parakei hot Baths at Helensville the next day.

In one two-week stage, we went to four balls at the Peter Pan Cabaret. I had two different partners, Graeme, three. One I had taken to the first ball. That fortnight included two nights footy training each week, game Saturday, then sailing club, and one trip to Parakei. I would hate to think how much beer we drank and the cost of it all. As I mentioned earlier – bullet proof.

Our wild lifestyle was soon to change – Graeme started courting my sister Marion. After going to Whitianga for Christmas, New Year 1956-57 with some mates, it was back to work for me, then two weeks annual CMT training at Linton Camp, then back to work and the start of football training. One day at work I heard Lynne telling one of the other office girls that her and her friend Margaret were going to the Wednesday night dance at St. Seps in Khyber Pass. Somehow, I also turned up, danced with Lynne and offered to drive the two girls home to New Lynn. That was the end of my 'Freedom days,' and the beginning of a friendship and love affair that except for one four-month break, when I ran off the rails, has lasted to the present day.

Back then I was twenty and Lynne only a few weeks away from 'sweet sixteen.' Easter was late that year. As it approached, Lynne asked me if I would like to go to the family bach. I said yes, then asked where it was. You could have knocked me down with a feather when she replied, 'Onetangi.'

The Beatty Bach was in the middle of a bush section. It was twenty-eight foot long and twelve feet wide, divided by two bunk rooms, containing four bunks at each end – men to the left, women to the right. In the middle was a combined dining room/kitchen that had a folding table, small bench and sink, a floor to ceiling safe with a cupboard above, plus a wood stove, and no power - one of the last to be connected. We used a primus for cooking and kero lamps for light. A long seat ran from wall to wall at the front window. There was a long drop outside.

Eight of us went down for that weekend, a full house. Alan,

Lynne's dad and his mate went down on the 2pm sailing. The rest of us left on the 6pm *Baroona* from King's Wharf, now the container terminal. At Ostend it was a mad scramble on to Clarry Thompson's old bus for the trip to Onetangi. The bus was packed, every seat taken, no standing room left, jam-packed to the rafters. The bus rattled and swayed on the metal road as it made its way to Onetangi.

I was hanging on as best I could, my reasonably sized weekend bag between my feet. The first stop was Trig Hill Road, and the first guy off was one of the first on. He had sat on the back seat and struggled to get past the standing passengers and their luggage. Beside the driver was a large box for bags, mostly suitcases, or big framed packs (few of the soft bags of today), of course he had a large suitcase at the bottom of the box. Finally, he got off. It was a good five-minute stop.

Thankfully our stop was the next one, Paterson's Corner. We headed up the hill, past Crocker's Store, and walked for ten minutes to Hobson Terrace. Finally, we got to number thrity-two and climbed up the bank, along the darkened track, one behind the other, to the bach. At least the lamps had been lit.

We unpacked, opened a welcome beer (room temperature) then prepared dinner and went to bed reasonably early. It had been a long day. The weekend was a continuous party. Saturday night we piled on to Tommy Paterson's truck (Alan in cab) and drove off to some guy's place in Ostend. Sunday night we had visitors for a singsong, Tex Grbic and Guitar, the leader, his younger brother later married Lynne's sister Jill. That weekender was to be the forerunner of many more weekends.

Kids and Characters

1957 was to be a big and memorable year for me. Lynne and I started a lifelong relationship and I turned twenty-one. We had a small party at home with my family and the Beatty family, plus a few footie mates and their girlfriends. On the following Friday, four of us from our Point Chev rugby league team boarded the *Waveanella* for the four-day sailing to Sydney as part of the Auckland under twenty-one rep sides tour of NSW.

Right from the start of the year, I had set my sights on making the tour and started training early to be the fittest I could get. As the season progressed, I played some of my best ever club games. I also went well during the four-week trials process to be selected. Our unbeaten four-match tour, was followed by a win over an Auckland team on our return. It was a great experience. We had flown back to Auckland in a teal (now AIRNZ) DC3, a six-hour flight.

The previous Christmas before teaming up with Lynne, four of us Point Boys had gone camping at Whitianga. Previously we had gone to Orewa. We had a good time, so booked again for the following Christmas. However, two pulled out at the last minute, leaving only Mac and I to go. On New Years Day (1958), Mac and I agreed we had had enough and returned to Auckland. I also had an ulterior motive.

We arrived back at Point Chev early in the afternoon. I parked the car off the road, unpacked the tent, emptied my bag, and repacked it with shorts, footy Jersey, two T-shirts, a jumper, togs, beach towels and pyjamas. I added a few cans of spag, plus fruit and eight bottles of beer. I left a note for Mum: 'Off up road. Bus to King's Wharf for late sailing to Ostend.'

I went down to the *Baroona* fo'c'sle, sitting there was Eddie, Lynne's uncle who at that stage I had only met briefly. That was to start a life-long friendship until his sad death from cancer in 1991. Eddie was ten years older than me but we were both Leos. He was a devoted rugby man and me a league man, yet we got on well together. At that stage, he was working on trucks for the post office mailroom. He had worked through the Christmas and New Year period and was starting his holidays.

When we arrived at Hobson Terrace, Eddie said to me, 'Lead the way to see how you would've got on if you were on your own'. I hadn't been to the bach since that previous Easter. I found the track to the bach. As we got closer, he said he would go in first. He gave the usual whistle to let them know. The door opened to his knock. As he went in, he said 'I've got Norm with me.' They all thought that was a mate of his. When I entered, they all got a surprise. Thankfully, Lynne was pleased to see me. Eddie went on up to his bach.

Over the following years, except 1960, both before and after our marriage, Christmas Holidays were spent at the bach where I got to know many of the local families. The first was Tom and Dot Paterson's children Ronnie, Raewyn, Kevin and Bruce. Dot had claimed part of Tommy's garage for a drapery-cum-gift-shop. Over the years she expanded to virtually take over the whole garage. Dot's Drapery became a great place for everything from beachwear to every game available.

In 1958 we arrived Christmas Eve morning. In the afternoon I went in to buy Lynne's Christmas present. I'm sure Dot had a telepathic sense. Although there was no-one else in the shop, she ignored me, flitting around, rearranging items on the shelves until a lady came in, then she stopped and said, 'Hi, Norm, looking for something for Lynne?'

I nodded.

Dot reached down into a drawer to pull out an orange-coloured shortie nightie, holding it up to show it off, she said, 'Will this do? Look, you can see right through it.' Dot put the nightie on the counter, held up her cupped hands. 'She's about this size, isn't she?'

I blushed, she had set me up beautifully. After that year, it became a regular game. But she never made me blush again.

Dot had a great sense of humour. She was always laughing and loved a good joke. Over the years I became prepared and would always have one ready for her. Those holidays, Lynne and I would walk to the beach after lunch. Waiting on the Patersons' back steps would be Kevin (seven years old) and Bruce (five years old) in togs with towels, no hats or shoes. Dot had told them to wait for us and go to the beach with us. On the way we would pass the Kupa house on the corner of Fourth Ave and Waiheke Road where the youngest two, Arthur (Arfa) and Eva would join in. Once on the beach the three Jump boys, from a Māori family, plus the Partridge kids would join our crew. When we hit the water, the kids would climb all over us. We would pick them up to toss them high into the sea. They loved it and we had fun.

One day Arfa said to us very seriously, 'People would think you were our Mummy and Daddy.'

Keeping a straight face, I replied. 'I don't think so Arfa, we've got different suntans.'

Over the latter years I became great mates with Kevin. Sadly, they have both passed away. I gave Eulogies at both their funerals. At Dot's, I had the great pleasure of recalling our first Christmas present encounter.

In those pre-Pub days, and before we married, Lynne and I often went to the bach with her dad, Alan, for summer and holiday weekends. Alan usually went down on the early sailing; we went on the later boat. We travelled light as we left spare clothing and beach gear at the bach. I worked in the city. On the Thursday, I would order and pay for one dozen beers to be delivered to Waiheke. On Fridays, on my way to the boat, I would collect steak and chops from downtown Hellaby's Butcher. On walking up to the bach, we passed Crocker's Store where Merv stayed open on Friday nights to cater for the last boat arrivals and to collect other needed items.

At the bach we would unpack, have dinner and settle in. It was always a lottery as to whether Alan was home or out on 'walkabout'. At this stage, Alan was better known as 'Doddery', a nickname given to him by Waiheke's first All Black, Adrian Clarke, a family friend. Adrian had attended the high school when it was held at the Onetangi Hall which doubled as a store.

On Saturday mornings Alan would have breakfast, then take off, arriving back when he felt like it. Alan had a small duffle bag known as his 'Bludgers Bag'. He would fill it up with a couple of my bottles of beer, magazine, paper backs and the odd items someone had requested he collect for them. First stop would be the Patersons where he usually swapped paperbacks. Then on to Ned and Iris Davis where it was books for veges. Then to Farley and Mavis Scott's where again he unloaded spoils brought with him or procured on the way for whatever the Scotts had to offer. By the time he got back, the bag would only contain a few items. That was Doddery's way - give it away.

Saturday nights it was either off again or stay home to play cards, Coon Can or Monopoly. On a couple of occasions, we had some odd happenings when Alan came home. On one, we were playing cards when we heard him calling 'Norm, Norm'. He had got off the track and was stumbling around in the bush. I went out with the big torch. He wanted me to stand at the corner of the bach to shine the torch in his direction, which he was able to follow, crashing and swearing until finally in view.

One hot February night when Alan had gone walkabout, Lynne and I after dinner were sitting at the table. We heard someone approaching the bach door. The front window was open. I called out, no answer, then we heard the intruder stumble over a pile of bottles stacked to one side. Silence, again I called out. It was obviously not a friendly visitor. I said to Lynne, I would go out to see if I could see them.

'No way,' she said in a rather panicky tone. She didn't want to be left alone inside. Around that period there had been several properties broken into by a well-known local alkie with only liquor being stolen. He was not a nice man, and we were sure he was our unwanted caller. Lynne was quite frightened. She insisted I lock the back door and placed a chair under the door handle. When we were ready to hit our bunks, Alan hadn't returned and Lynne was still scared. She insisted I sleep in the girls' room, she in top bunk, me in the bottom. Of course, we went to sleep. Later there was banging on the door that woke both of us. I leapt out of the bunk fearing the guy had returned. Lynne was in a panic. It was Doddery yelling, 'What's going on in there?' With relief I unlocked the door. I quickly told him what had transpired. Thankfully he accepted the story. The alkie was arrested a few weeks later.

Lynne and I went on one of Doddery's walkabouts one Saturday morning. We visited the three families then left him at Scott's. He arrived home several hours later having made a few calls on the way home.

Over those years I got to know the Scott boys well, Blake, Gordon, who boarded with Mrs. Beatty during his apprenticeship years and wife Sally, Phil and Gaylene. I knew Neville, Raewyn and Karen Davis and of course the Paterson lot.

Good people with plenty of character.

The Pub and the Sheriff

The opening of the Onetangi Hotel and Wholesale was on the last Saturday of September 1959. Built of the corner on the Strand and Third Ave, it was a separate building constructed on land owned by the La Franchie family where the private hotel has stood, and still stands today. The La Franchies had obtained a license through Dominion Breweries (DB). Before the Hotel started business, locals and bach owners either made homebrew (some good, some awful) or had their supplies sent from the city.

Vern was an easy-going publican. A trait he had, was when smoking a cigarette, he would place it in the right-hand corner of his mouth and would point it to the left under his nose, very odd. It was the days of 9am opening to 6pm closing and the famed 'six o'clock swill.' The last hour would be a race to drink as much beer as possible before the closing bell was rung.

Beer was served in eight ounce and five ounce (lady's waist) glasses, rum, whiskey, gin and brandy were the only spirits and were served in a shot glass. Patrons added the water, ginger ale or cloves that were provided on the bar top. Women were not allowed in the bar and had to use the lounge area. This rule was lifted a few years later.

Surprisingly, some of these women swore more than the men, using the 'F' word regularly. Men never swore in general conversation as they do today. Swearing is now commonplace for both sexes, even on TV, once taboo.

One of the barmen, an ex-pom, was always well presented in his black longs, white shirt and bow tie. He was dark haired with swarthy skin, dark eyes, and a small moustache. He looked more Greek than English. Before the pub got too crowded, he would spot you coming in, and by the time you got to the bar he would have your drinks poured and ready.

The pub also ran a delivery service all over the island on a Saturday. Orders had to be placed by lunchtime, and they were then delivered by pub-truck in the afternoon. Food was not available (except pies from a warmer). Often Vern would put on a 'pub-lunch' of leftovers from the private hotel kitchen.

There was always the usual crew that arrived early morning. Before the first race of the day, Vern would place a 'best bets' on the bar. Patrons would pick a number, mark it, and pay a shilling. It was all quiet when the pub radio broadcast the race. The winner who took all the money, usually shouted and still made a profit. This usually lasted about three races before the crowd got too big.

One Saturday morning, a Scottish guy who lived in Second Ave, won the first two races, and shouted twice. A couple of weeks later he came into the bar as the patrons were selecting bets for the first race. In a loud broad voice he said, 'Where were you lot when I fell in the creek the other week. There I was all alone, pulling the water around me to keep me warm. No, you were all here drinking me beer.' It was greeted with much laughter.

In the afternoon it was darts, sixpence in, highest score takes all. The marker called your name when your turn came up. If you didn't get to the score line by the second call, you were out, no refund for not making it. The winner became scorer for next game. On Saturdays, one win could pay for your day. I am only an average player and didn't always partake. On one occasion, I had a win, the only one.

There were some very good players, plus a few characters. Ted was one, dressed in a suit, no tie, pork pie hat, threw a dart like a spear, then jumped up and down after he had thrown, he wasn't too bad. Another was Bill, a local farmer with a glass eye. He was the first man I ever saw that had his ears pierced and he would hang a dart from each ear. Bill was a heavy drinker; at his farmhouse he had hidden bottles of whiskey in many secret spots. One night Eddie and I were having a beer with him at the farmhouse and Bill produced a bottle of whiskey. When you had a sip, he would pour a nip into your beer glass when you were not looking. One had to be wide-awake, or your glass would finish up half full of spirit, not a nice taste.

Eddie did several stints as a barman over the years. One Labour Weekend in the early sixties, I went to stay with him. On the Friday night he told me they were one barman short for Saturday afternoon and I was to be the replacement. This was a new experience for me. The bar was a semi-circle, with one barman working from one corner, the other barmen operated the other half. The cash till was in the middle.

The barman used a 'gun' attached to a hose. He held the glass on an angle, pushed hard on the trigger, directing the flow to the higher side of the glass, and then gradually straightening the glass to an upright position, leaving a small head at the top. It was a knack that had to be mastered, and it took a bit of practice to achieve.

I started at 2pm before the bar got busy. At 3pm, the bus that started at Oneroa, picking up passengers from Palm Beach, Surfdale and Ostend, arrived. Thirsty patrons swarmed into the pub. Eddie and I were non-stop pouring beer. I poured one patron's beer and he just stood there looking at the glass, then at me. He said, 'You working for the publican?' The head on his beer slightly higher than it should've been. I topped it up. Later we became good friends. His name was Bob Stouppe and he drove the council grader. One Christmas I was having a beer with him and I mentioned the Council hadn't graded Hobson Terrace for a while and my Morris Minor was scraping the bottom on the ridge formed in the centre of the road. He replied, 'No problem, I start back on Monday.' Sure enough, Monday rolled around, the scraper came and flattened our road.

Barmen used to smoke back then, as did most patrons; they also drank while they were behind the Bar. I didn't smoke and refrained from having a beer. I was too busy to make a hash of my job. At closing time, a well-known local, Ross Day, said to me, 'Norm, it's a pleasure to see a sober barman at 6pm.' I was flattered. After clean-up we sat around until about 8pm having all the beer we wanted.

On the Monday before catching the bus, I called into the pub. Vern handed me a bundle of notes, folded around some coins. I wasn't really expecting anything. He said, 'You work, you get paid.'

The following year I was commandeered again. That was the first year of 10pm closing. Vern had doubled the size of the lounge and added a small-sized shed, the 'Jug Bar' outside in the beer garden area. This was only for beer in jugs, one price, easy to run. That was my job and I started at 4pm. It was a breeze. At 8pm Vern collapsed into a seat behind me. He stated he had done his bit for the day. He sat there smoking, with a beer and chatted to me. At evening's end, it was usual for a few beers, then Monday, a handful of money.

On weekends when I stayed with Eddie and he worked in the pub, at 6pm he would hand me a cloth to clean the tables, or Vern gave me the till to count and record takings for him, very trusting. There was no way I was likely to take anything; I enjoyed the free beer afterwards. Ah, great days.

There was only one policeman on the island, with assistance from the city at holiday times. In this period the cop was Noel Brennan 'the Sheriff,' the best cop the island ever had. Noel was the old type of cop, but fair. He knew everyone and would take troublesome teens home to their parents and give both a strong lecture.

On one occasion he took a youngster home that had been causing quite a lot of trouble. He told the father, the next time it would be straight to the lock up for the night. The father, surprised Noel when he replied, 'Take him tonight, it might wake him up.' Noel did. The young guy never got into trouble again.

On Saturday pub days, the Sheriff would come into the bar area before closing, talk to the locals, and at last bell after they had left, he would hang up his hat, then Vern would serve him a beer. One day Eddie asked him about the under-age guys drinking in the Bar. Noel replied, 'I would rather them in here under control, than out on the beach causing trouble. Anyway, most of them are better behaved than their dads.'

The Sheriff would meet most boats from the city (three). If anyone looked an 'unlikely' type, he would inform them they weren't wanted on the island and put them back on the boat to return to the city. Imagine a cop trying this tactic today. The cop would be suspended for police harassment.

Strange Sea Trips on Waitemata

Over the years, I have had some strange trips on our beautiful Waitemata Harbour. One anniversary weekend, Lynne and I were on the Friday 6pm sailing on the Baroona to Ostend. Allan, who usually caught the earlier sailing had missed it and was up in the wheelhouse when we boarded.

Allan was wharf foreman for a big Auckland cartage company. He knew all the skippers and never paid a fare. At King's Wharf, he would walk straight on, then up to the wheelhouse. On return from Ostend, he went to the end of the wharf, caught the rope thrown from the ferry, placed it around the wharf bollard, then stepped on.

Allan called us up to the wheelhouse. It was a clear evening, the boat packed with passengers. As the boat passed North Head with Bean Rock close by to the right, the captain, Bill, (not his real name) said to me, 'Here, take the wheel. When we get close to the white marker on the rocks off Motuihe, keep well clear to the left and call me.'

Bill and Allan went into the small cabin behind to have a beer. I had never steered a craft of any kind, not even a P. class yacht. Half an hour later Bill re-appeared and took over. No one was ever the wiser. Imagine that happening in this day of health-and-safety. I love telling this story – I assure the reader it is true.

Later that year at Queen's Birthday weekend, Lynne had played hockey while I had played footie on the Saturday. We decided to go to the bach on the early Sunday sailing. As we boarded the Baroona, Bill invited Lynne and I up to the wheelhouse. He told us it was to be a long day for him as he was to go to Surfdale first, then Ostend, then on to the bottom end. I had gotten to know Bill quite well as he was a keen rugby league man and often went to Carlaw Park.

I had never been to Surfdale Wharf, and when we berthed, he asked me to help him put the gangway up as the tide was dead low. Once in place it was very steep, the small lot leaving went very slowly, struggling with their luggage. Bill was getting red faced and ruffled. In a very loud voice he bellowed, 'You're like Brown's bloody cows, if you don't get moving, we'll be stuck on the bottom for hours.'

This got the desired effect; they were soon off. Back in the wheelhouse Bill grabbed the wheel, and instructed the engineer to go full steam ahead. We took off like in a Grand Prix start. Brown mud churned up around the boat. We bumped the bottom several times but were on our way to Ostend.

1960 was not a good year for me. My downhill slide started on Anniversary Day. It was a Monday. I had spent more time with Eddie than Lynne. Mid-afternoon we decided to go to the pub for a few farewell beers, then catch the 5pm Bus to Ostend. Tommy Paterson came into the bar, he said he would take us over in his van as he had luggage to take to the wharf. We agreed - bad decision.

Around 5.30pm we left the bar and reached the wharf soon after. A young guy approached Tommy and asked him where his dog was as they were not allowed on the bus. Tommy had forgotten it. As the *Baroona* was not in view, Tommy suggested to the guy we go back and get it and that we might as well go for the ride. We agreed —my worst decision of the year. I should have gotten off to catch up with Lynne who was waiting on the wharf.

On the way back, just past Seaview Road at Ostend, Tommy skidded on some loose metal down the bank, somehow finishing up on the driver's side. How any of us weren't seriously injured I'll never know. I was the worst off. We had been sitting on the long seat (no belts) behind the driver. His seat was held in place by a floor to ceiling pole, and there was no passenger seat.

I had hit the pole, probably lucky as I could have shot through the front window. I broke my collar bone and was covered in blood from a bad head cut. The others only had minor treatable injuries. I went off in an ambulance to Surfdale, then Freddie Ladd's widgeon to Mechanic's Bay, then by Ambulance to Auckland Hospital.

Lynne was not happy with me. She had looked for me on the boat to no avail. As Alan and Lynne disembarked, someone from the ferry office told Alan I was in the emergency ward at Auckland Hospital. Alan went home to New Lynn and Lynne came straight to the emergency ward. I had been cleaned up, my collar bone strapped back and discharged. But I was not a pretty sight. My light blue polo shirt was covered in blood. I was obviously intoxicated and having an argument with a nurse who would not let me ring my father to pick me up. This was the scenario when she arrived.

Finally, I was allowed a phone call. Dad picked us up, dropped me home, then took Lynne to New Lynn. I'd dodged a bullet and should've learned my lesson as Lynne was going to give me the 'Heave ho'. I didn't. The injury meant I was unable to play footy. I trained with the team to finally get cleared to play the last two games of the season.

Eddie and I meanwhile, went to the island every third weekend for a boozy time. We had also spent our Sundays back in the city sanding and painting a two-man yacht we had purchased to sail to Onetangi, and to leave it there for future pleasure.

I stopped spending time with Lynne, apart from a few Saturday and Wednesday night movies. By early September she had had enough, so gave me the boot. Deep down, I knew I was in the wrong. My injury, no footie and general mood, plus too much booze was my downfall.

Eddie and my big adventure to sail our boat to the island was set for Labour Weekend Saturday. Eddie had the yacht picked up then delivered to Okahu Bay on a post office truck. He had arranged for some of our personal gear to be delivered to Merv Crocker's Store in a mail bag, courtesy again of the post office. I spent the Friday night at Eddies.

Early on Saturday morning we taxied to Okahu Bay, dragged the yacht alongside the wharf to the first set of steps where Eddie was to step the mast. The first disaster came when Eddie, moving around, unsettled and rocked the boat. He fell in the water up to his waist. Finally, with the mast in place and all adjustments completed, we set sail, Eddie on the tiller, me forward. With mainsail and jib up we were away on my first sailing adventure.

Norm (aka Artie) 23 and Eddie (aka Snow) 33 at New Lynn, November 1959. In the fictional stories they are twenty years apart instead of ten so Artie was the same age as Snow's fictional son, John.

We made good time to get to the eastern end of Motuihe where we were to make the big decision to continue around to the bottom end, or turn left around Oneroa to sail triumphantly into Onetangi Bay. The decision was made for us. Eddie needed a whizz, stood up, and the boat jibed sharply, bringing the mast down with all the sails.

We recovered all the gear on board, but the tide was taking us past Crusoe Island. The *Muritai* came into view, it appeared to change course toward us, then continued on its path to Matiatia. I think they saw Eddie drinking a beer, and decided that we didn't need to be rescued. As we drifted, we attached the jib to the spinnaker pole, as we came to the opening to Matiatia, Eddie steered us in. We dropped the sail and took to the paddles I had insisted on carrying.

Slowly we headed to the beach, pulled the boat up, stored all the gear in a pile, turned the boat upside down, secured it, then caught a taxi to Eddy's, picking our gear up at Merv's on the way.

In the afternoon we went to the pub, no mention was made of our morning's epic saga. We were met by our mates who told us we were lucky to have not been on the *Baroona* the previous night as the cops had raided the fo'c'sle.

The next time we came to the island we decided to take the yacht out in the bay. Tommy had picked up the boat and delivered it to Farley Scott's place. We got the yacht all shipshape and into the sea we went. The first small wave tipped us out. We beached the boat then donated it to the Waiheke Sea Scouts. Like Burl Ives's popular song, 'Red Sails in the Sunset' – I'll go sailing no more - I haven't!

Reconciliation

In the months after Lynne and I split up and the Labour Weekend yacht saga, I was at a loose end. I missed Lynne. It took me awhile to get over it, knowing I had stuffed up. It was my fault.

I went to Onetangi with Eddie every second weekend. One Saturday night I went to the Point Chevalier Sailing Club Dance. I felt like a fish out of water. There was no male or female I knew. A younger crowd made me feel ten years older. I left early and walked home. Sundays weren't so bad; I would bike down to Coyle Park at Point Chev. Beach to play touch footie with a big group of locals, mostly local rugby league players of all ages.

By Christmas I had given up on any hope of luring Lynne back. I knew she was enjoying her newfound freedom. I went to Eddie's for the holidays, over the next ten days, we had several drifters who came and went. Colin, Lynne's cousin, stayed for a week. It was a boozy time. We usually hit the beach after lunch, had a swim, then pub time, out at 6pm, home for dinner, play cards.

Lynne and I had only spoken on a few occasions at the beach and the New Year's Eve dance. After the New Year holiday was over and all the drifters had gone their merry ways, Eddie's older brother, Barry, wife Daphne, and two kids, came to spend the next two weeks at the bach.

Although Eddie's and the Beatty's Bach backed onto each other, neither Lynne, nor I had visited. On the Thursday Lynne and her friend Ethel had come up to Eddie's in the early evening to see her uncle Barry and family. They had called in as they were going back to town the next day; Lynne was going to the Saturday Grand Prix with her new beau and his mates.

When they were ready to leave, it was dark. The girls didn't have torches. Daphne very graciously asked me to take the big torch to help them through the bush. Being the gentleman, I agreed. Lynne went first as she had been on that track many times. Ethel was next with me at the rear shining the torch forward so they could see. As we got close to the bach, Ethel took off, passed Lynne, and shot in the back door then closed it behind her, leaving Lynne and I alone outside. We had a short chat, then agreed to keep in touch. I told her I was seriously thinking of going to Sydney, to the Bondi area where I had been billeted during my 1957 Auckland under-tewnty-one rugby league trip. I told her there was nothing for me to stay.

I rang Lynne on the following Monday when I started back to work. I asked her how the Grand Prix went? She floored me when she replied she didn't go and had broken off with the guy. She agreed to go with me to the Wednesday night movie at the New Lynn Delta Theatre. After that date when we got back to her place, and had a kiss and cuddle, we decided to get back together. After that decision was made I said, 'If we're going to get back together, we may as well get married.' Lynne instantly said 'Yes.' That was it, no bended knee, no build up, proposal, agreement – probably the quickest wedding proposal on record.

We made the decision not to tell anyone as Margaret, the Beattys daughter was to marry on the Saturday in a fortnight's time. We didn't want to spoil her big day. On the Friday night, we went to Bronson's Jeweler on Queen Street, who was having a closing down sale (it lasted two years). There was fifty percent off all engagement rings. Lynne selected one for twenty-five pounds. The salesman also sold us the wedding ring for six pounds, all up thirty-one pounds, the equivalent of three weeks pay for me. At that time all our mates purchased their rings at Bronson's.

On the Sunday morning after Margaret's wedding, I went to the Beattys. Lynne and I told them we were getting married. They were quite happy. After all, except for about four months, we had served a four-year 'apprenticeship.' They asked us when the big day was to be. We answered as soon as we could arrange it. Finding a wedding reception place was impossible as the March-April timeline was every year's busiest time. After many phone calls my Point Chev. Club's hall was available for the eighteenth of March, the only date available. We booked knowing we would have to do our own catering.

That was not a problem as Mum's family had been in catering since way back in the 1930s when they had run a home cookery in Te Puke. Elsie, Grace and Mum were in charge. I paid for the hall, band and beer. Dad paid for wine and spirits. Lynne's mum made the wedding dress and going away outfit, plus two bridesmaids' and flower girls' frocks.

One week before the wedding, Lynne celebrated her twentieth birthday at home with a small party and we were married on Saturday the eighteenth of March 1961, 4pm at New Lynn's St. Thomas Anglican Church by Reverend King (though I was a Presbyterian). After the wedding it was off to have photos, followed by the reception in Point Chevalier.

Later in the evening we went back to my place to change and pick up a rental car. Back for the traditional farewell, then to the Royal Hotel Honeymoon Suite on the corner of Victoria and Elliot Streets. Ironically, it was opposite to the Macky Logan Building where we first met, exactly five years before on Lynne's first day of work. Next morning, it was back home for some clothes and food left over from the wedding.

Lynne's boss had lent us their family bach at Glinks Gully, a west coast beach south of Dargaville. We stayed three days then went on to Paihia. Friday it was back to New Lynn, our home for the next three years. Saturday, I played in a club trial game, then on Monday went to Waiheke for a couple of of quiet days. On Thursday the mob arrived for Easter – men to the left, women to the right.

Honeymoon over.

At that stage I was a shipping clerk at National Trading. A few months previously, one of the sales staff left under a cloud. I applied for his job, but the general manager told me it had been filled; he didn't seem all that impressed that I wanted to improve myself. I got the impression I was getting pigeonholed.

At a party a few weeks after we were married, I was talking to a guy who worked for a leading NZ export company that had recently broken into the new Japanese market. The company had added a one-man importing section as the Japanese were sending them products to on-sell. I applied and was taken on. It meant a slight rise in my earnings.

We hadn't planned on children but were not worried if it happened. It did and we purchased a section. A house was to be built on it for a parade of homes. We had to turn it down as the mortgage was over our budget and the sales job was stop-go. One morning Ray gave me a pair of binoculars plus a case sent from Japan to see what interest we would get. I left the Anzac Avenue office and went up one side of Queen Street, Karangahape Road, then down the other side of Queen Street, up Victoria Street to Meltzer's who ordered six a pair. I then walked along Fort St and called into A.H. Nathans. I walked out with an order for a hundred. Back at the office, everyone, including the big boss congratulated me on the sales. I had made my years' salary on one day. I thought they might do the decent thing, maybe at least a bonus or a week's pay. Nothing. At that stage I couldn't see us getting a house anytime soon.

A few mornings later, a Thursday, Ray gave me some papers to deliver to a Quay St. company. I walked out of the office and never returned. I delivered the papers, went to the post office and sent a telegram to my workplace: 'Please accept immediate resignation'. I then caught the bus back to New Lynn, changed out of my suit and tie, then went up to the brickworks who were always advertising for staff.

In the afternoon when Lynne came home, heavily pregnant, she was surprised to see me. 'What are you doing home?'

I replied, 'I've thrown in my job,' then quickly added, 'I've got a job at the brickworks.'

On Monday the fourth of November, I started at the six-week-old Stahlton flooring plant, not knowing I would spend the next thirty plus years working under the Ceramco banner. Lynne who had worked only five minutes from home, gave up her job eight weeks before Keith was born at Grey Lynn Salvation Army at 6am on the eleventh of December. I was present at the birth and saw the mid-wife beat the doctor to the delivery. Lynne stayed twelve days, the normal period back then. On the day they came home, I went to the matron's office and paid the account. The matron carried the baby to the car, put Keith on Lynne's lap and wished us all the best. We were home for Christmas, our new family.

1961 had been a busy year. I started single, then got engaged, then married. I had played a full footie season, worked three different jobs from clerical to labourer. I then topped the year by becoming a father. It was a very memorable year.

Slow Boat to Waiheke

The ferry, *Kestrel*, must have plied its trade on the Waitemata for the best part of a century. I had been on it to Devonport as a lad. I had also made many trips on it from the Ferry Buildings to Matiatia. It was on an anniversary weekend and I was to make a very unusual journey.

After my holiday with family at Christmas, my son, Keith, fourteen, at the time, had come back to the city when I returned to work. He was to compete in the Auckland swimming champs. He finished on the Friday evening and on a very hot Saturday morning we boarded *the Kestrel*. It was packed with weekenders and day-trippers. We had to sit on the deck in front of the wheelhouse.

As we passed Devonport, I heard a commotion behind us. I stood up to see a woman yelling at the skipper to turn around, her husband was in a bad way. The skipper was trying to explain he couldn't leave the wheelhouse and there was only the engineer down below and the deckhand on board.

I told him I would go and have a look for him. Luckily the guy was just inside the door of the top deck cabin. He was slumped out of his seat on the floor. He was grey, blood coming from his mouth down his shirt. I went straight back to inform the skipper he would have to turn back.

He replied he would go on to Matiatia to get help there, I told him that would be too late, that the guy, who I guessed to be in his fifties, would be dead by then. I said to call up for an ambulance to meet us at the Devonport wharf. His reply absolutely stunned me; the ferry didn't have a radio.

I told him I would climb up on top of the ferry to flag down one of the many launches that were heading out into the gulf. I asked the passengers on the front deck not to wave then clambered onto the roof of the ferry. I waved at a launch that was level with us. The skipper waved back and continued on. The skipper of the next launch saw me and noticed the ferry was in reverse. He drew up beside the ferry and I shouted across waves, asking him to call for an Ambulance to meet us at Devonport. He gave me the thumbs up. We turned around, unloaded the sick man to the ambulance, and then continued on to Matiatia.

Lynne and Sandra were waiting for us when we finally berthed, well over an hour late, like everyone else, no one on the wharf had any idea of the drama we had been through. On the way back to Onetangi, Lynne spotted her sister Gaye and her husband's launch, anchored close in the bay. We turned into the car park as they came out of the store. We were just starting to have a catch up with them when somebody said, 'You're the guy that was the on the roof of the ferry!' It was the guy that had radioed for the ambulance. I told them the story. He and his family were anchored right next to our family.

That afternoon in the Onetangi Pub I relayed the story to council chairman, Jack McIntosh, telling him about the lack of a radio. I would send them a letter. He told me he had a drawer full of complaints about the ferry to write to the Marine Department. The reply I got from the Marine Department was rather short, stating that the ferry wasn't required to carry a radio because it was licensed on a river ticket.

Several years later, on a very dark winter night, Lynne and I were returning to Waiheke on *the Kestrel*. I was reminded of that earlier scenario as I looked out of the *Kestrel's* windows. There were no lights to be seen as we approached the gap at the heads of Matiatia

Bay. The ferry slowed down to slower than slow. 'I could walk faster than this tub is going,' I remarked to Lynne. Finally, we saw the lights on the wharf and were glad to disembark.

Once on the safety of the bus I said to Lynne, 'Imagine if we had hit the Motuhihe reef and gone down, no-one would've known. They would probably assume the Kestrel was just later than usual.' It would probably have taken a couple of hours before anyone would have had any idea there had been a disaster. No launches were out on that black night.

As the *Kestrel* got further into old age, it got even slower. I recall coming back from the island one summer Sunday evening. When we were passing North Head. Lynne's mum, Joyce, remarked, 'I'm sure we have already passed North Head.' That trip took two hours. One Sunday night coming home on a very packed Kestrel I went down into the engine room, and sat on a bench seat to have a beer with the stoker who was shoveling coal into the hot box of the boiler to create the steam to drive the engines.

When the fast boats came onto the scene, the Kestrel was retired to be converted into a floating restaurant berthed in the Ferry Basin. Later it sunk, was refloated, and towed to a resting place in the upper harbour. I'm not sure of its final destination but have a feeling it was sold for scrap.

Car Jerry Capers

My first experience of bringing a car to Waiheke was when we brought our Morris Minor over in the mid sixties. I had to deliver it to Subristzky's yard in Pakuranga and leave it there. They drove it to Half Moon Bay to the barge, which was then to be towed by tug. My dad then picked me up and took me to the ferry buildings to catch up with Lynne and the kids for the *Baroona* to Matiatia.

By the time we arrived, the cars were all in the parking Area. They had just completed loading cars from Waiheke to go to the city and were pulling out. As we were getting into our car, I noticed a guy running along the wharf waving his arms and shouting to the tug. His car had been taken off the barge but had been re-loaded. I don't know what happened in the end. I guess the tug would've been obligated to turn back.

A couple of years later we had our first Bach delivered to Waiheke. Several factors converged for us to achieve what would normally take many years. Firstly, the area where the Beatty house had stood in New Lynn was re-zoned commercial, then Alan died, leaving only Mrs. Beatty and her boarder, Gordon Scott, in residence.

Joyce made the decision to gift the front part of the house to Lynne and I. It contained a large bedroom that we turned into a bedroom, sitting room, lounge and kitchen area. It had a small bedroom, plus the passage area to the front door. We sealed this area converting it into a narrow bunkroom for Keith and a mate and we demolished the porch.

Joyce contracted James Davern, the premier house movers of the day to separate the two areas and move them apart. This allowed a footie mate, Terry Sisson, to help me to re-frame and clad the two open areas which we achieved over several weekends. Then a date was set for the big move. Davern came the afternoon before take-off, jacked up the bach on to a trailer, cut the top part of the roof down to go under power lines, and chained the bach to the trailer – ready to go.

There were four men in the crew. The foreman said I could go with them, so I slept in the house the night before leaving. They arrived at 3am, hooked the trailer to an articulated truck, then drove off into the night. Our convoy was police car with flashing lights in front, afterwhich came the winch truck with two of the crew, loaded with everything they would need on site. The truck and trailer followed with the foreman, one crewman and me.

We travelled through Mt. Roskill, Penrose, down Great South Road, over Panmure Bridge to Half Moon Bay, then on to the barge. We all piled on to the tug. As daylight slowly arrived we were already leaving the Tamaki River. One of the boys went down to the galley re-appearing with bacon and eggs, plus hot coffee. We settled down for the trip to Matiatia where the traffic cop would be waiting.

As we passed Music Point, the foreman said to his crew they should try out the new ramp at Kennedy Point that had only recently been built. One of his guys reminded him the traffic cop would be at Matiatia. The foreman wasn't worried about that. He reckoned that the day was fine, there was no wind, and it would be high tide – decision made.

The landing was smooth. We were unofficially the first house removal to arrive at Kennedy Point. As no one had previously gone on that road, two of the crew had to get up on the roof to cut back any branches that were impeding our way. They also had a long pole with a flat board on top to prop any power lines that crossed the road. We moved slowly along Donald Bruce Road to the junction with the main road. Then it was off to Onetangi.

At the junction of Eden Terrace and Victoria Road, the winch truck replaced the articulated truck to tow the house up the hillside to the building site that Colin Aspen had levelled out for me. Luckily, there were no other baches on the Hobson Terrace area of our site. As we went over the drain at the bottom of the hill, two of the crew placed an empty fourty-gallon drum under the trailer to stop it from rocking. Once the trailer was on site, the boss made me check the position to confirm the bach was in the right place, the house was jacked up and sitting on blocks, the trailer was taken away.

After lunch they dug out the holes with a petrol-driven post-hole-borer, and put the foundation poles in place. A petrol driven mixer was used to mix metal and cement to fill the holes. All this gear and supplies had been on the back of the winch truck. After that it was knock off time, and on to the pub for beer and dinner. I went with them and shouted. They stayed the night at the pub. I slept in our first bach.

They returned the next morning, lowered the bach onto the foundations and secured them. They also put the roof back to its original position. It was all finished by lunchtime, and they left for the city. I went back to the city on the last sailing. Terry and I returned the next weekend, the last before Christmas to complete the last jobs. I had arranged for Jimmy Lockie to complete the electricity work. He agreed to get it done and arranged with the power board to have it connected.

On Saturday afternoon in the pub, Eddie introduced me to the foreman of the power board. He confirmed the job would be done and I shouted him a beer. I returned on Friday's 6am Christmas Eve sailing, car packed with gear and Christmas presents. I opened the door, switched down the light switch – no power – bugger! I unpacked the car in record time and raced over to the power board in Ostend.

I asked a guy very politely, 'Number six Hobson Terrace, the power was to be connected?' He picked up a clipboard, looked at me and replied. 'Yes, that's been done, did you check the main, we don't leave it turned on.' Trust me, the obvious answer. Even a dumbo like me should have worked that out.

Out the door I bolted, by now sweat was pouring down my face and back. I drove, full speed back to Onetangi, opened the door, switched on the main, and heard the purring sound of a fridge going. I turned a light switch. There was light. What a feeling of relief. At last, we would have a Christmas with cold beer, milk and kids' drinks, plus a freezer full of supplies.

The time was ticking and it was close to picking up Lynne and the kids, and friends from the boat. I grabbed four bottles of beer and headed off. I called in at the power board, the team were starting to knock off. As I gave the guy the beer I said, 'You've made our Christmas, big thank you.' Then I got to the wharf just as the boat was berthing. It was a very happy lot when I was to answer Lynne's first question, 'Is the power on?' with an emphatic 'Yes!' before I told her the whole story.

That Christmas Eve's 6am sailing to Kennedy Point, was to become a ritual. For many years there were four of us on the same sailing. Alec Arnott, a workmate at Ceramco, Duncan McRae, a 1956 Kiwi to Australia, who played for the same club as me, and Peter Fell, who like me retired to the island, a man I was to have a lot of time with, a great guy. Sadly, all have passed away over the past few years.

Over the years the car ferries have got bigger, better and faster, plus more sailings. They now also carry passengers. All the island's supplies are carried down in containers towed by artics, plus trucks packed with building materials and supplies. The island now has mostly sealed roads, many cars and even double-decker buses.

I must tell one last tale against myself. After one work Christmas-break-up-party, I arrived home late and 'slightly' inebriated. Lynne was not too happy as I wasn't in any condition to load the car. I promised to do it in the morning. Next morning, I was up at 4.30am to pack the car, I left Glen Eden at 5am for the Half Moon Bay check in at 6am. Then, with luck, I would be off to Waiheke. I had to make the sailing. If we missed it, it might be several days before we would get another one. I made the sailing but on the way over, I wasn't feeling too great, I had to wind the windows down to get in as much fresh air as possible.

on site Hobson Tce

landing at K.P.

Roy Dog's Holiday

Two months after Keith's family pet dog, Roy, died, Keith and I were going through a box of his possessions. There was his favourite tennis ball, shredded down to the leather, the bone he used to chew on, a few lengths of red ribbon that had come off Christmas presents, plus a small pair of Emily's red socks that had gone missing.

At the bottom of the box was a diary he had secretly written of his holiday with me at Onetangi, March to April 2007, when his family of Keith, Jane, Samuel (seventeen) and Emily (fourteen) went to Europe for six weeks. At the same time Lynne went to Brisbane for the birth of Jackson to Sarndra and Brandon.

Keith and I read the diary and laughed all the way through as Roy told his daily story. At the end was a footnote: *Hi Norm, loved our holiday. Can you please break the dairy down into one of those short stories you are always writing? Put it in a competition if you win have a beer on me. Thanks, love you all. Roy Dog.* Here is that story in the words of Roy Dog.

Keith and Jane had told me of their trip. Also, that Lynne would be away. I was to stay with Norm. I was quite happy with that. I always enjoyed my weekends and holidays at Onetangi. I always got on well with Norm. He's not a bad guy for an 'oldie.'

Jane took me down to the island. Two days later Norm and I took Lynne over to the boat on her way to Brizzie. Back at the bach, Norm looked at me and said 'Dog,' my real name is Roy, but when he was serious or annoyed, he would always point to my bed in the corner adding 'sin bin.' He said, 'Dog, its you and me against the world.' I didn't really understand, just wagged my tail.

Norm is a man of routine. Every day it was out of bed by eight. At night I snuked up on to his bed and snuggled into his back. After breakfast he would open the terrace door, say, 'Car.' Then off I would go, wait for him to open my door, then slide on to the passengers' seat, where I sat bolt upright waiting for the day's adventure to start.

We went off down Seventh Ave to the car park. As soon as Norm opened my door it was off to the beach for my daily walk and toilet stop. Free from my lead, our usual routine was to head towards the western end rocks. Norm was having a serious knee problem. He would stop about sixty yards short of the rocks where I would go to the toilet. I would stop, then look around to see Norm who would be calling me. I ignored him.

Cunning old Norm, he would walk away not looking back. Then I would sprint up to his side, he just smiled at me. At the eastern end we went through the same drama. I'm a male spoodle, a cross between a spaniel and a poodle. Our breed is known to be slightly disobedient. I fit the bill to a tee. I enjoy it. I'm also as black as coal. Often, we ran across the same people and their dogs. There was one lovely lady and her white female poodle. We stopped to chat each day. I was a bit worried there might be more to it, on Norm's side, than just a fleeting meeting on the beach. I thought I might have to report to Lynne when she came back. But later realized it was a casual meeting.

For my part, I quite fancied the poodle, but my lot had done something to me to curb my ideas, if you know what I mean. But I still liked to imagine what we may have produced – maybe a dog with black and white squares like that famous Pommie rugby club? I made Norm blush one day while we were talking to them. I spied a sandcastle, pyramid shaped. I casually walked over, lifted my left leg, then peed on its peak, watching it roll down. Then I backed up, squatted, and let a bomb go. By the time it had rolled to the bottom I was in fits of laughter. Norm was red as, he said, 'Time to go,' then gave me a dirty look as we left the scene.

Another day as we neared the ramp to exit the beach, I spied an Asian family sitting on a blanket preparing their lunch. Great, I love food! Off I went and circled them, tongue out. Norm was yelling, telling them not to give me any food and for me to 'Get

Norm and Roy, July 2005

here!' After a couple more circles with Norm close behind, I took off up the ramp to wait by the car like an obedient dog. Norm came up, opened the door, said, 'Get in.' I missed the sin bin that time.

I loved those runs along the beach. Once Norm had a long stick with a scoop on one end, he put a ball in it, then threw it down the beach. I chased after it, grabbing it while it was still bouncing, then ran back to Norm. I dutifully placed it on the sand in front of him, and then made eye contact with him as he moved to pick to pick it up. I beat him to it, then ran away, ball in my mouth. For some reason Norm never brought the ball again.

Norm used to hide a stick under the ramp. He would throw it along the sand, or into the sea. That was great. I'd run in to the sea, swim out bring the stick back to Norm, but he was too quick for me. When I had dropped the stick, he quickly put his foot on it and grabbed it. It's probably still under the ramp.

As we left the beach to drive along the Strand, I would sit in the passenger seat, and Norm called me the navigator. When I saw a dog, I barked at it. Norm would tell me to stop. I kept barking until we had passed it. A couple of times I noticed Norm looking at a couple of young things in bikinis on the beach. I looked at him and barked. He just smiled.

Next stop was to collect the Herald from the petrol station where there was a lovely blonde lady called Jackie. She was a very dog friendly but sadly died of cancer at a young age. When Jackie came to talk to me through the open window while she pumped petrol, I always barked at her. Sorry lady. You don't touch my car when I'm in it. However, on Sundays we always walked to the service station via Seaview Road and that was a different story. As Norm went into the shop, Jackie would come out, pat me, and tell me I was a good dog. Then it was a walk along the beach, up Seventh Ave and home.

On those days I hated, Norm was always ready for me. On our return from the beach, Norm tied my lead around the foot of a heavy, iron framed garden seat. Out came the hose, full bucket of warm soapy water and a scrubbing brush. When Norm was finished, I always shook myself close to him, revenge. He then towelled me down. I loved that. He left me tied up for the final drip dry.

Every Tuesday after lunch, Norm, and his mate Johnny Mac, played golf. And one time Norm took me along. He thought it would be good for me to have a run around, as there were only a few other golfers out there. Norm teed-off. I chased the ball and brought it back to him. Norm was not impressed. He tied my lead to his golf cart. I was never invited again.

The next time he went, he locked me inside the bach. But I remembered he had put some lamb chop bones in the kitchen tidy. I tipped it over. The bones fell out. They were good, my favourite, although I'm not supposed to eat them. When Norm came home, I snuggled up against his leg, then he spotted the mess I'd left, he yelled, 'Dog, sin bin!' I slumped off.

The following week, he thought he was cunning. He put the bin in the plastic clothesbasket and placed it on top of the washing machine. As soon as he left, I went out to the laundry, jumped up, got my paw into one of the holes in the basket and pulled the whole lot on to the floor. Ah, my favourite meal again. It was the same scenario when Norm arrived home I made a fuss of him, then, 'Dog, sin bin!' again. He beat me the next weeks, he put the bin on top of the lavatory and closed the door. No more bones.

Norm's pub days were Thursday and Saturday, 4pm on the dot, then home by 6.30pm. The first time we went, he took me in to the beer garden, sat me under his stool at the leaner table. Everything was fine until a guy brought his mutt into the beer garden. I did my usual barking act. Norm put me back in the car. From then on, Norm left me in the car, window down enough for fresh air. I either sat on the floor or up in his driver's seat. When he was ready to go, if I was in his seat, he would say, 'Move over. I'm the driver. You, Dog, are the navigator.' Most afternoons Inga would come out for a chat and bring me a bowl of water, a nice lady. Friday night was RSA night. He left me at home and came back by 7.30pm to see Coro Street, some TV soap he never missed.

My favourite antic that always got Norm into a lather was at night, when it got dark, to paw on the door as if I needed a pee. Norm would open the door and watch me. As soon as he looked away, I would shoot off behind the house. I knew once I disappeared, he couldn't see me as I was as black as the night and invisible.

I would go along the back path behind the next two houses, then down to the road via the steep driveway. I would re-appear under the streetlight at the elbow bend and stand there casually looking back up the road. Norm would be standing there yelling 'Roy, get here!' over and over. When he spotted me, I would walk slowly up the road keeping close to the bank so he couldn't see me, finally emerging at the bottom of the driveway, I then crept ever so slowly on to the terrace. The usual 'sin bin' would follow.

One night I was away over half an hour. Norm was not pleased. When I arrived back, he grabbed my collar put the lead on and tied me to the garden seat, shut the door to leave me outside in the cold. I was a very good dog when he let me free. The holiday finally ended. We went to Matiatia to collect Lynne. She made a fuss of me. I had to sit in the back but stood up to put my nose between the two front seats. Two days later Lynne took me to the ferry buildings to meet Jane. It was then home to Avondale, the family, and the prezzies, plus the usual carry on about their trip.

Over the years I've often thought of that holiday with Norm. We got on well. We had a great time. I remember his send off when Lynne and I went to the boat, he leaned on the car door, patted me and said, 'See ya around, mate.' He called me mate. I felt a small tear. Yeah, he wasn't too bad for an oldie.

Roy died aged fifteen, a very good age for a spoodle. He was cremated and his ashes spread into the sea of Onetangi Beach, opposite the ramp from the car park at the bottom of Seventh Ave. And yes, Dog, we had a great time, we all love you and miss you. Norm.

Falling Trees at Hobson Terrace

The Beatty family owned three sections on Hobson Terrace. Eddie Smith, Joyce Beatty's younger brother, owned three sections on Trig Hill Road. These sections backed on to each other. This was the case going down the two roads. That middle area was thick with all types of native trees, untouched for many years. It was very dense. People just didn't venture there, except the odd cannabis grower whose secret patches were well clear of prying eyes.

In between, and to the downward side of the valley where the two families had their baches was a massive puriri tree, about sixty feet high, and I guess well over a thousand years old. It took pride of place when looking out over Eddie's front window toward Ostend, standing high over all the other vegetation.

One day, I think in the seventies, Eddie looked out and was surprised to see the usual sight was gone. The puriri had fallen. There were few people living in the area at the time. No one had heard it. Eddie went to the area where there was only a stump. The tree had rotted just above it, then sheared off. The fall had taken out several other native trees and pongas. The trunk is probably lying where it fell all those years ago. I know no effort was ever made to clear it up.

After Joyce Beatty died, her oldest daughter, Anne, inherited the bach. In the early nineties Anne asked me to look at the puriri tree growing on their section, between the road and the bach. It was around thirty feet high; it had been there when Joyce purchased the section.

The tree had a big hole at about chest height from the ground. It was hollow inside and filled with black, dirty water. I told Anne it should be taken down, as if it fell it could hit the bach, or cross the road taking out all the power lines, plus whatever else was in its path. I told her she should get advice as soon as possible. The tree was not healthy. There were quite a few people present when this discussion was happening. One woman, the type who knows everything, was most adamant that it should be left. The tree was fine. Nothing was done.The next time Anne and her husband George went to Onetangi, the tree had fallen, blocking the track to the bach. Fortunately, the damage done was light, just several ponga and a few saplings. Anne had the tree removed by contractors.

In 1980 Lynne and I decided we wanted to move from Hobson Tce to somewhere nearer the sea. On Easter Friday, Tom Johnson, one of the few local Agents, showed us several Onetangi sites. As soon as we saw, and inspected, twenty-two Seventh Ave, a hundred yards from the beach and with magnificent views we agreed this was it. It is still in the family.

The purchase price was $20,000, which equated to one year of my salary as a production manager. It consisted of three rooms upstairs, a dining and kitchen area, a bedroom/sitting room, and a small bunkroom. Downstairs was a narrow bunkroom, which ran the width of the bach. There was also a small laundry area and a shower, luxury at last, even hot water.

The first thing we installed was a wood burner box stove. Overtime we added a laundry, flush toilet, and a shower, plus a back porch at the rear. In 1986, before taking off on our big OE, we extended the downstairs area into a self-contained unit. Later adding a toilet.

During 1987, we had a concrete septic tank installed by Cliff Schaffer. Also, a 5000-gallon concrete water tank was built on site at the back of the section by Dave Tong. The tank was a massive job as the boys had to barrow the mixed concrete down from Seaview Road. Dave reckoned it was the steepest site he had ever encountered.

The costs of the septic and water tanks were each $2,500. Both were paid by courtesy of the TAB as twice that year I had won over $3,000 on three-dollar trifectas (I used racing skill and knowledge to pick my winners). In those days, the Saturday Herald published a horoscope, which contained your lucky number for the week. Easy, I took Lynne's and my number then picked who I thought was going to win the days main race, there's your trifecta. How's that for skill.

Finally in 2001 we demolished the top area to completely rebuild it. We also extended the outside terrace area. All the materials had to be carried up from driveways: timber, gib-board, fibro sheets, roofing iron, everything. Outside, I constructed several retaining walls, posthole boring the clay for posts deep into the ground, and then nailing half rounds in to retain the ground. Our daughter Sarndra called it the 'half-round-house' the posts were all concreted in, and a perforated hose placed behind the wall.

I also mixed the concrete by hand in a wheelbarrow for all the posts, plus the steps and paths I made for both sides and the back path. For the concrete blocks I laid four foundations inside the bottom area. I also painted the outside of the bach three times. I did most of the inside painting as well. We only got painters in for finishing the upstairs area when it was rebuilt. As I've mentioned, everything had to be carried, and I was the number one labourer. No wonder my back is now stuffed. From the time of that car crash back in 1961, I've had neck and back problems, also my time labouring at Brickworks certainly didn't help, nor the fact that I played footie until I was thirty-four.

In October 2011 I had a right knee replacement caused by a football injury that originally occurred way back in 1958. Dr. Bond warned me that would be the end of my weed-eating on our steep section as a slip could prove disastrous. By 2015 at age seventy-nine, I was starting to feel the effects from several problems, so we decided to look at retirement homes. It took four months to finally make our decision to go to the Waiheke Retirement Village in Ostend. Returning to the first place we looked at. We moved in on twenty-fifth of November, a decision we've never regretted. For me it was the right time.

Falling Trees at Seventh Ave

When we took over at Seventh Ave, the previous owners had obviously never done much work outside. The front area facing the road was full of Agapanthus – great for holding up the bank. A grass track ran up to the back door of the bach. There were a couple of hibiscus trees and a pohutukawa on the boundary with next-door neighbour.

Forest Gold 1980

On the other side, next to the reserve were a karo, a cabbage tree, and a pohutukawa, which was a mystery for several years, as it never came out in flower. It even had Gordon Scott and wife, Sally, baffled, and they were horticulturists by trade. Several years later at Christmas, one flower appeared, next year, four. The third year it came out in full bloom, which it repeated yearly ever after. It was also the last pohutukawa to bloom in Onetangi. Where others had lost their colour for the festive season, ours remained in full bloom.

The back part of the section had a lone pohutukawa, which we never touched, behind the existing concrete tank. We also had a thirty-foot high macracapa, which my mate Jim and I cut down over one Easter weekend. I used a lot of the lower branches to retain an area behind it that had slipped and left a rather gaping gap in the ground then filled it with foliage from the tree.

In the area between the reserve, and us a dozen pines, each about ten feet high had been planted. I envisaged how high they would get, too high in my opinion, so down they came, there was the odd tree here and there, plus two very high pines planted on the berm from Seaview Road. These had been planted to denote the back pegs. The back area was also covered in honeysuckle. Removing the honey suckle was a task. We took the advice of TV garden host, Eion Scarrow, and cut the creeper back as far as possible, letting the plant flower, then spot spraying to kill the roots. It worked.

In the flat area to the side adjourning the reserve, the only thing standing was the long-drop dunny, which I was to shift three times, until it was right on the reserve boundary. It is still standing. This area I gradually developed over the years - making it several sizes bigger.

At the front of the area, I built a strong retaining wall behind the pohutukawa. It ran from the bach to the reserve next to the dunny. Here, I placed a small tin garden shed. Where I retained the bank, I built an outdoor barbeque out of small rocks from the beach. The fire area I covered with firebricks, I had a small chimney with a bend, cut from a copper pipe. I then placed the barbeque plate over it. Many a barbeque was had there. Nowadays it is illegal.

Over time we added an outdoor garden table with seats that sat six. A birdie bath and a macrocapa chopping block took up the area. I started a vege garden behind the wall. The bottom was clay, I filled it with chopped seaweed and horse poo, all free of charge. The horses would leave me plenty on their way to the beach. I also built a potting area.

In this area, I spent many happy hours potting, then re-potting seedlings and small trees. I had karo, koromiko, karaka, hebes, hibiscus and pohutukawa. Many I planted out on my section, others I gave away. There are a number of my pohutukawa going well around the island. My one regret, despite all effort, was I couldn't get kowhai going. I had a vege garden and grew carnations. Lynne had a rose garden and still has them at the village.

There had been a major slip in the area around 1963. There was minor damage at our place. But next door it had taken a large chunk out of the back area, making it impossible to access their section from Seaview Road. Three sections down, the house slipped from its foundations to slide down the hill, coming to a rest against a tree. It was re-located on the site. Only to later burn to the ground.

A house owned by Poppy Quilter which was close to the beach was completely destroyed and a woman resident killed. The back of the next door property was a wilderness of scruffy trees dominated by a massive macrocarpa. When a severe northerly storm hit the tree was slightly uprooted and fell facing Seaview Road. It was on a fourty-five degree angle off the ground. No one worried about the tree, as it was obvious at some stage, it would unbalance and fall the way it was pointing to the road. Wrong. One stormy Friday night just after the millennium around midnight, there was an almighty crash right outside our recently built bedroom.

I opened the door out to the small north-facing terrace. The macrocarpa had fallen between the two houses. It had also missed, by inches, bringing down the power lines from our bach to the power pole on the road. It had knocked out several karo trees I had planted close to the boundary. Neither house was damaged, but the mess of broken trees and branches next door was massive. The stump of the tree was leaning toward the sea, leaving a hole behind it big enough for a man to stand up in.

The neighbour hired a contractor to clean the area up. He cut up all the larger branches into firewood sized lengths and sold them. He milled as much of the trunk on site into building lengths, then left the site. I offered to clean it up, no charge. In return I got three years firewood out of it. The clean up took me about three months. Around this time whenever I went for a swim, I would look up towards the two pine trees at the back of our section. On Seaview Road between the two trees was a lamppost that always made me liken it to the three wickets at a cricket match.

Slowly over time I noticed the wicket on the right gave the impression it was moving outwards. At this stage I was also having worries about the giant macrocarpa in the reserve behind my dunny. It had a massive trunk. I imagine it would take four men, clasping hands to circumnavigate it. Two separate trunks grew out of it to about sixty feet high.

Looking at it from the terrace, I had the impression it was also on the move. There were also the three pine trees close to it. I hand delivered a letter to the local council pointing out the possible danger if the back pines or the macrocarpa fell. The council arborist came to inspect the trees. He informed me all five pine trees were to be felled as they were diseased. He said the macrocarpa was ok, and if it fell it would probably fall towards the sea. I looked him straight in the eye and said, 'Come with me. I'll show you a tree that didn't fall the way it was expected to.'

I took him up to the neighbour's stump: told him the story and said, 'Trees don't always fall the way you expect them to. They have a mind of their own.'

He assured me I had no problems. Two months later I was back on to the council. In my opinion the macrocarpa was on the move. The arborist came back, again he reassured me everything was ok. One week later I was proved right. Around daylight there was a tremendous bang. The house shook. It sounded like a bomb had landed. Lynne and I both shot upright.

'What was that?' Lynne asked.

'I think we've had a lightning strike on the roof,' I replied.

Lynne said, 'No, I have broken glass over me.'

The glass was a few small pieces that had been knocked out of the stained glass window that originated from the Beatty's New Lynn home. We had put it in the bach when we shipped it down, then on to the new Seventh Ave property, a family heirloom. I jumped out of bed and opened the back door to be greeted by the top of the macrocarpa filling the area. It was lying along the path that ran behind the bach. In the fall, the tree had missed the dunny, demolished the shed, taken out the back half of the pohutukawa, missed the concrete water tank, stripped all the plumbing off the back wall, and damaged three sheets of roofing iron.

At 7am I ran the park supervisor, he arrived soon after. Around 8am contractors for the council arrived to start the massive clean up. Later a lovely young lady, who had been appointed as liaison officer by the council arrived. She was brilliant. My son, Keith, who had his own helicopter business arrived. He had landed in the reserve next to the youth hostel. He had a photo showing the tree had actually split in two, the other half falling in the reserve.

The council spent a week on site. They left me a good supply to cut up for firewood. They removed all foliage and unwanted trees. They also took the entire demolished shed away. I was able to retrieve all my tools and gear, plus most of my sporting mementos that had adorned the walls.

The liaison lady had apologized for the arborist. He was off work with the flu. The next week he turned up with a bottle of wine. He offered his most profuse apologies. He was expecting the *I told you so* bullet. Lynne and I surprised him. I smiled. We shook hands. I just said, 'I told you trees had a mind of their own.'

Over time we did all the repairs, and had the garden shed rebuilt. The pohutukawa tree took about three years to get back to its original state. I've often upset people when I state that they are like weeds. But they are. They grow anywhere. They grow out of cracks in the cliff side. They flourish without any help, relying only on nature. Their root system goes as far, as they are high. The hairs on the roots get into sewerage systems then expand to fill the whole pipe or system. Believe me, I have plenty of experience in dealing with the problem. The blooms clog the spouting. It is a must to keep waterways clear. I needed to clear our spouting three to four times a year.

I'm aware of protestors and tree huggers that often want to stop a developer (fair enough). However when they want to stop diseased trees from being felled, they should leave it to the experts. I remember a case in Rotorua where there was a big protest to stop a big ash tree from coming down. They won their case. But in the end it fell, crushed a car and killed the driver. When the macrocarpa fell, it was the closest I've ever been to meeting my maker; a few feet separated us from extinction. Yes, trees have a mind of their own, and I love pohutukawas – my favourite tree.

My Mate Kev

My mate Kevin Paterson, Kev, could've been the main character in one of my favourite author, Barry Crump's, books. You know the type of guy, you knew, or after a few pages completely understood the guy Crump was writing about. Kev was brought up, and went to school on the island. The Patersons were well known. On leaving school, Kev tried farming, then worked as a kitchen hand in a big Auckland hotel. After that he went back to the island to drive a truck

Kevin Paterson, Onetangi Beach Races - 2009

for his dad's carrying company, later taken over by Subritzky's. He then chose a life on the sea as a fisherman.

Kev married, had two children, got a house in Glenfield and continued as a fisherman. Later he divorced and returned to his parent's house at Onetangi. He purchased a tractor, plus all the gear for contracting work around the island. He also owned a tinny with an outboard motor for fishing. He smoked fish and sold it.

Another of Kev's pursuits was pulling down old lampposts to get the copper wire out of the telephone lines, which he would then sell. It was on one of these days when he was scavenging on the seventh fairway of the golf course that disaster struck. The lamppost Kev was pulling down slewed around and slammed across his legs. He managed to untangle himself to fall to the ground laying there for ages before a golfer found him and made the call for help.

Kev was airlifted to the hospital (it was even splashed over the Herald). The decision was made to save his leg over amputation. It was a decision that Kev would agonise over in later life. Whenever it became painful, he would say to me, 'I wish they had've cut the bloody thing off.' After a long hospital stay, it was home to the island for a long recuperation.

Alcohol was never far from Kev's hand. He had always lived in the alcohol fuelled company of booze, beer and the seaman's demon rum, these being the main components of his diet. The minute he got out of bed, he would open a small bottle of Lion Red. Then, after a small breakfast, he would head out to the garage. I used to call in when I went to get the Herald, and he would be sitting on the woodblock, beer in hand, working on a tractor, or sometimes chopping wood. Around lunchtime, which he never had, he would call in to my place when I would indulge in my first homebrew of the day. Then off he would go to Johnny Mac's for another taste of homebrew, before calling into the pub for a top up. After that it was home for a snooze, sometimes returning to the pub for the workers' hour.

To mix things up he sometimes reversed the procedure, starting at Johnny Mac's. One afternoon he left the pub and called into

Eddie's Store (now a restaurant) to get a packet of tobacco. When he came out, the local cop, Alf, was leaning against his back wheel. Alf said, 'You're not going to drive that home are you, Kevin,' Kev replied, 'No, but you'll have to take me home as I can't walk that far.' Alf did. Kev walked back later and drove the tractor home.

Kev was one of those fix it guys. He could fix anything, electric, plumbing, kitchen appliances, and car motors. His specialty was tractor motors and their punctures.

I had known Kev from the time I first started coming to Onetangi with Lynne. The Beatties and the Patersons were life-long friends. We were always up to date with all the news of their four children. Kev was one of that group of kids that came to the beach. In his mid-teens, when he came to the pub, I had a beer with him. When I retired in 1992, we became close mates.

In 2001 after Lynne had decided to retire, we had the top part of our bach demolished and builders rebuilt the area to be more modern. During this stage Kev and I built an eight-foot by six foot garden shed with a woodshed behind it out of the demolition timber and offcuts and anything we could bludge (like a window).

Norm, Kev, Mark, the shed, Norm's birthday lunch, August 2005

We were very proud that the overall cost to me was only 115 dollars, plus homebrew and a few packets of tobacco. The only materials we purchased were six concrete foundation blocks, a couple of bags of Redimix cement mix and two tubes of glue for the window. Not bad, eh? Kev would turn up around nine every morning, and then finish at our lunchtime.

Kev followed the same routine when I painted the finished house, , always with a beer in hand of course. One Sunday after the shed was completed, we had a special lunch to commemorate the opening of the shed. Our whole family came down.

Our granddaughter, Emily, nine at the time, wrote and read out an ode to Norm and Kevin's shed. It took pride of place on the inside wall. Jane, our daughter in law, couldn't believe that Kev got up onto the scaffold to paint. She was surprised that Kev didn't eat anything at lunchtime. In the end she put food on a plate and gave it to him. He ate it.

Sometimes Kev would turn up around 4pm, my beer time. We would sit outside the shed telling stories of our diverse lives. The tuis and pidgeons would settle in the nearby pohutukawa tree, listening to us. Sometimes they would dive on to the side of the birdie bath to have a drink. The tuis often also had a bath, sending water flying.

Kevin's health slowly downgraded, he didn't go out in his tinny as he had trouble getting into the water. He grew a long beard to hide his cancer growth. But he held off going to the doctor. Finally, one morning, Dot called the ambulance. I went to see him off. Defiantly, he got into the passenger seat, he wouldn't get in the back. That was the last time I saw him. He died in hospital a week later. He didn't make it to sixty.

I gave the eulogy at his funeral. I reminded people that many of them there had Kevin fix something for them. I reminded them of his cheeky smile. The older women all loved him. I made light of his drinking. He was a lovable rogue. After me, a lifelong mate and schoolmate, Wally Ngapo, summed it up better than me. 'Kevin had his demons,' he said. It was a sad day.

I missed Kevin for a long time, the cheeky grin, the sound of the tractor coming down the road, his days as a fisherman. The sight of him coming up the drive with a parcel wrapped in newspaper under his arm, knowing it would be a lunch of freshly smoked fish, still warm and ready for eating. Yes, Kev was a great mate, one that Barry Crump would have been proud to use as a character in one of his stories.

THE SHED

When Norm and Kevin built the shed they didn't shop, at
Placemakers INSTEAD
They pillaged and borrowed and begged their way
through, there was nothing this team couldn't do.

Each day they toiled this wonderous crew,
Spurred on by Lynne's bread rolls and the magic home
brew

And this is the result this brilliant shed
Of silver and blue and purple and red
(Well it would be if I had painted it)
But Norm says "it always pays to be modest, when it
comes to building a shed"

When Kevin and Norm had finished the shed,
They didn't just pack up their things INSTEAD
They invited the neighbours and half of the street
To a shed warming party with plenty to eat.

And Norm and Kevin smiled proudly and said
**NOW THAT'S WHAT I CALL
A SPECTACULAR SHED......**

By Emily Stephens (age 11)   15th August 2004
Norm's Granddaughter

Island Solo Cops

For many years the policeman on the island was a solo cop, with assistance at holiday times. The best was the Sheriff, Noel Brennen, whom I've already mentioned. But possibly the biggest man to take office was Lyndsay Proctor, an Ellerslie Club prop forward, who I knew through my position of Premier grade coach for Glenora. Lyndsay was also a teammate of the current island plumber, Mike Dodds. And he also mowed the Mad Butcher's lawns in Onetangi.

When I retired in 1992, the cop was a young Samoan guy, whose name eludes me. I had cause to call him as I was getting malicious phone calls and knew who was doing them. It came to a head one Sunday when I was expecting a call from Lynne to tell me her sister, who was in the last part of her life with cancer, had passed away. Annoyingly, I received three calls from people who had placed adverts in the Gulf News for selling certain items with the same story – 'You rang me yesterday to say if I didn't sell the item to ring back on Sunday. I apologized and advised them of what was happening. I also asked, 'Did the guy speak like an Aussie?' all three answered yes.

I outlined my suspicions to the cop. We decided on Plan A, for him to speak to John, I never received another call. Plan B, that had my daughter in law Jane worried, was to knock on his door, when he opened it to plant my right fist on to his beaky nose.

Probably the last single cop was Alf, the smallest. I was taller than him, but he was well built and could obviously handle himself. One late Sunday morning, Mark and I decided to play nine holes of golf. We met up with Alf who was on his own. When we finished Mark invited him to my place for a home brew. Surprisingly, he came. He arrived about 1pm in his own vehicle. He told us he was going to dinner that night with a lovely young lady. The afternoon turned into a 'session.' Mark left at 5pm. I reminded Alf about his date. He left soon after. Some weeks later I asked him how the dinner went. He replied, 'Good.' I didn't ask him about his driving.

A few weeks later, on the Saturday before Christmas, Mark, Lynne and I went to a barbeque at Mike Dodd's Surfdale home. We left around midnight. As we came up to the sports club, Lynne, who was the 'sober' driver, said, 'The police car is up ahead.' When Lynne reached Belgium Street, she said, 'The cop car is behind me, the lights are flashing.' She pulled over. Alf appeared at her open window, 'Where's your DG license?' Lynne thought he had said driver's license. 'No, your dangerous goods license, you're carrying two of them.' Alf then wished us a goodnight, then went back to his car laughing no doubt. We laughed too.

Alf was probably the last of the solo cops, a pity in many ways, as they knew everyone, and all knew them. Some had families who went to school here, some were involved in local groups and a couple played for the local league team. I didn't know a bad one.

Many Changes in My Time

In the seventy-five years I've been coming to Waiheke Island, I've seen many changes. There has always been a divided population. Those who want progress, those who don't, those that want the grass to grow opposed to those who don't. When I first came down, there were a handful of rich farmers and maybe the odd city businessman. Now I reckon there are more millionaires per square acre than anywhere else in New Zealand.

Over years (not in chronological order) I have witnessed many changes, the rock and roll era through to flower power and free love (Oh dear!). When I first came to the island in 1957, all villages, Oneroa (the biggest), Surfdale, Ostend, Palm Beach and Onetangi had at least one general store, a post office, some combined, some a petrol station. Oneroa had the only bowling club, a movie theatre (now the Red Cross), a dairy, fish-n-chip-shop, hardware store, Bob Burns' wine shop, plus a few other shops. All five areas had a public hall that had dances over the holiday periods. They were also used by the various local communities. There was an annual flower and garden competition at the Morra Hall.

All areas had at least one church of various denominations. The Masons and the Buffs had lodges. There was one cop stationed in Oneroa, an ambulance service, volunteer fire service, about three doctors, plus a handful of land agents. Most areas were serviced by locally owned carriers. The roads were metal, the lifestyle quiet. There were no liquor outlets only Bob Burns' wineshop, plus Gridiska Vineyards where the bus station now stands. The wine sold was known as plonk, the worst I've ever tasted.

One Labour weekend on a Sunday after a seven-a-side rugby tournament at the area school, our lot poured into the 'closed' back of Tommy Paterson's van to have a party at Onetangi. About 8pm we ran out of beer. Tommy took up a collection and 'ran the cutter' to Ostend for four bottles of plonk. About midnight Eddie and I fell asleep at Tommy's. I woke with a headache, toothache and gut ache. Man, I was crook. First thing in the morning Tommy and Eddie, plus a few stragglers, opened a beer. Not for me, no way. Tommy went out to the van, returning with a full flagon. 'Anyone want this?' he said. To everyone's surprise, I said I'd have it. Tommy handed it to me. I took it outside and poured it out on the lawn. When I went back inside, I said, 'No one's going to drink that, and, Tom, you probably won't need to mow that patch anymore.'

There were Primary schools at Blackpool and Ostend, later combined into an area school that took in high school students who previously had to go to the city. There are now two primary schools, a high school plus kindergarten, the combined number of pupils possibly as large as the whole island population of the late fifties.

There was also a big change in shipping to the island. The island's Surfdale, Ostend and Rocky Bay wharves were closed. The Ostend causeway was built. Baty's Bridge opened up Rocky Bay to the rest of the island. Goodbye to the *Tangaroa* and *Onewa*. The passenger service then went exclusively to Matiatia, three boats from the city each day, a worker's boat each working morning to the city. The *Muritai, Baroona* and *Motonui* provided the service. All other supplies came by scow or barge.

Those days no one envisaged that in seventy years' time the island would have: forty plus vineyards, some making world-class award-winning wines; many top-class olive groves; top New Zealand restaurants; that there would be fifty takeaway outlets of every type (except KFC); that there would be a large supermarket, bigger than any hall on the island, selling every brand of beer and wine imaginablel; plus banks; shops of all types; and a major Mitre 10 (now a Placemakers).

At the present time there are over fifty licensed land agents, several lawyers, and public accountants, plus every other service imaginable. No longer a one-stop police shop in front of a side street house, but a police station on the main street, highly manned by a full-time team of officers.

The island is served by a rescue helicopter service direct to Auckland Hospital and has a volunteer coast guard vessel at Matiatia wharf. A hospital at the former Waiheke County Council yards in Ostend has been mooted for the future. There are also three medical centres at Oneroa, Ostend and the Marae, plus a blood test station at Oneroa. In the old days it was just a handful of doctors, mostly working from home.

Sport has taken a major jump forward from the days of the sports club playing rugby one week and league the next week, with one netball team. Now there are separate rugby, league, soccer, netball, boys' cricket, baseball and swimming clubs competing in the city competitions. Instead of only one small sized field at the sports ground there are several. The biggest fields are the rugby and soccer fields at Rangihoua, a new field at Ostend, plus grounds at the high school.

The soccer club is the biggest club now on the island, catering for both male and female players and covering many age groups. The top men's team, which has a strong mix of South American born residents, won the 2021 division and promotion to the top northern division for 2022. There are also many other sports and recreation activities to cater to all ages on the island.

Harbour transport has also dramatically changed from slow boats making three trips a day, when most locals thought that would never change, to a brief period with a hydrofoil that spent more time out of the water than in it. Now we have fast catamarans doing up to nineteen trips a day, including about four early morning workers' sailings. The new port at Kennedy Point saw the end of tugs and scows and heralded the arrival of car ferries. They are now allowed to carry passengers. These boats carry trucks carrying containers and large loads catering for all island businesses.

The roads are mostly paved with many cars, sometimes it's like a busy day in the city. Massive mansions now fill many isolated bays and main areas. The days of the old army-hut bach gone. There are even two storey apartments. Houses that once went for five to twenty grand are now a million dollars or more. Yes, the changing face of the island. All progress!

Magnificent Views from Forest Gold

When we moved to our 'dream' bach at Queen's Birthday weekend 1980 on Seventh Ave, Onetangi, we took the name *Forest Gold* with us. It was the name of the Beatty house in New Lynn. The name came from a yacht Alan had skippered in the late 1930s. When we moved the front part of the house to Hobson Terrace the name went with us. Joyce (Lynne's mum) was happy for us to carry

Forest Gold, 2000, before final alterations

on the tradition. There was a lot of greenery around. Over the years I planted several shrubs in the front that bloomed yellow. It gave a real forest gold colour to the property.

The views from the front windows were magnificent. Looking to the West was Thompson's Point, Little Barrier Island, Chanel Rock, Great Barrier Island, the tip of Coromandel and its range running along. Then sweeping around the east was the Bottom End, Rooster Point (real name Te Whau point).

Forest Gold, view to east, Coromandel in the background

Our son Keith, who owns a helicopter business, would often ring to check what the visibility was like when flying to Mercury Island. The view was forever changing. There were lovely sunrises and sunsets. At holiday times we looked out at the lights from the masts of 200 boats or more in the bay on Thompson's Point side.

Dolphins sometimes played in the bay. One late Autumn Saturday they gave us a show to remember. From 11am to dark, they jumped and dived continuously attracting a large crowd. It was a once in a lifetime exhibition. Sometimes the water would be boiling with kahawai being chased by stingrays herding them into one of corners in the bay for a feeding frenzy. The odd orca was sometimes seen.

One unwanted sight was the red sea arriving around the point, slowly coming into the shore, this started early into the new century. It was algae bloom, a sign of global warming. We also had the sight of the horse mussels swept onto the beach to be left looking like a highway. It cost thousands of dollars to remove them. There was also a tsunami warning when people were cleared from the beach.

One Saturday night during out first Christmas holidays we watched a replay of the famous film, *Giant,* starring the late James Dean. When the film finished around midnight, we pulled the curtains to see all the Rooster Point area in lights. At first, we thought it must be a cruise ship, then ruled that out. It was a mystery. The lights appeared well above the water line. There was also the throbbing sound of engines. We thought it might even be a UFO. In the morning we got the answer. It was the Australian navy Aircraft carrier, Jervis Bay. The lights had been from the deck high, rising thirty feet or so off the water line. The motors of course were the giant generators needed to run the ship. We were to see the Jervis Bay many more times.

One lovely summer morning after breakfast I looked out to see three tall ships: *the Spirit of Adventure, the Spirit of NZ,* and *the Soren Larsson.* What a magnificent sight they were, and not a fizz boat in sight. It made me imagine I was back a hundred and fifty years ago.

The Maori waka that had sailed to Tahiti and back was also often in the bay. It was a great sight to see. Coming up to Christmas, Fullers often ran special early evening parties on their catamarans. They would come into the bay, if one of the sailing ships were in the bay, they would circle them, then speed away.

Then there were the shipwrecks. Lovely expensive yachts and launches washed up onto the beach, usually when unattended, their owners boozing elsewhere. They would lie there to be pounded by the sea, until they looked like a stranded whale, to break up and be to be towed off to the tip to be burnt. Most of the owners were insured and didn't care, what an attitude!

One time there was a stranded whale. It was a Saturday, the morning was fine and hot. Around lunchtime the mist came in and the whale arrived with it. Many people came to the whale's aid. A trench was dug, the whale kept wet by the people and the mist. Around 3pm the mist went away. The whale was helped by its army of saviours, hauled and pushed along the trench, back into the sea and away. Thankfully, not to return.

Then there were the Idiots. Ninty-nine percent of boaties would drive their vehicles, with the boat on the trailer, towards the sea, make a U-turn on the hard sand then back, release the boat, then drive off. One late Autumn Sunday after lunch, the day cold, a slight wind, the sea choppy we had a 1% guy with an IQ to match. He drove towards the sea. Two guys, two women and four kids got out of the station wagon. The guy was the car driver and obviously the leader. He was tall, skinny and wore a wet suit. The kids ranged from about twelve to fifteen. The kids were wearing life jackets, the adults not. Unbelievably 'Long John' got into his car, drove it straight into the water, turned left, and stopped, he was stuck. I was in fits of laughter, who could possibly be that stupid, trying a U-turn in the sea.

My mate Kev has pulled out many drivers with his tractor when the back wheels had gone off the hard. Another guy was Peter Buffalor's son-in-law, Drew. The family had been watching. Drew went to his rescue. Once out, the car and trailer parked higher up the beach, the whole eight got into the fourteen-foot runabout. The progress out was slow. The boat had very little freeboard and was low in the water. They headed out and around Thompson's Point. I didn't really think I would see them again, but an hour later they returned to the beach. Two adults and two kids alighted and walked straight up to the bus stop, none looking back, nor a word spoken. The body language was all I needed to see there had been problems. Long John then headed out, around Thompson point. Two hours later they returned, backed the car down, boat on trailer. Long John got into the car, gunned the engine only to see the back wheels go down in the soft sand. Drew pulled him out again. He was the only guy to ever get stuck twice in the same day.

One Boxing Day, a car backed an unusual looking yacht into the sea. It was about twelve feet and had a very wide beam, the boat looked oval in shape, it could've been home built and obviously the family's Christmas present. There was a dad, a boy fifteen, a girl twelve, all on the plump side. They got the sail up, managed to get over the small breakers and set off. Next time I looked they were about fifty yards past the breakers, capsized. All three of them were in the water, no life jackets. The man stayed with the boat. Later some guys came to his aid and towed him in. The boy swam straight in towards Seventh Ave. However, the girl, not the strongest of swimmers drifted along the beach towards Sixth Ave. She appeared to be in trouble, but I could see swimmers near her were aware of her plight and assisted her to shore. I never saw that lot again.

One lovely summer holiday morning, when the bay was packed with boats, I noticed a sleek forty foot yacht anchored close to the shore. It had a tall mast, so it must also have had a large keel. I had a feeling it should've been out further in deeper water. Also, I noticed that the nearest two launches were anchored ten yards further out and they didn't need as much water.

There were about eight on the yacht having 'elevensies,' all drinking cocktails and gin-and-tonic, not a stubby in sight. They looked more like socialites than yachties. Sure enough the yacht lurched to one side, the mast pointing at an angle and people slid sideward. A few cried out in disbelief. The yacht was stuck.

It is well known that yachties and launchies don't get on and no one came to their aid. A dinghy was launched, and several manoeuvres were attempted to tow the yacht out, but to no avail. Finally, a couple of runabouts managed to pull the yacht clear into deeper water. Inexperience was obviously the key to the near disaster.

Then there was Roger, the man who rowed the fastest dinghy in the West. Yes Roger, Roger of Gluttons fame, in his boat *Smellie Nellie*. Roger is well known as the guy who can dig holes and trenches where diggers can't reach. The man who does the hard work others turn away. No matter how rough the sea, Roger would row through it. It was a great sight to see him on top of a wave in complete control. I never saw him can out, once settled and past the waves, he would row so fast the dinghy had a wake behind him, like a small motor would've left. Then he'd head off across the bay to Rooster Point. If dinghy racing had been an Olympic sport Roger would've been a good bet for a gold medal.

We had many visitors and guests over the years, both locals and from overseas, including Lynne's British relatives (her mother was born in Gravesend, England). They all loved our bach and marvelled at our magnificent view.

Eventually, we left Onetangi for the Ostend Retirement Village and left our children to take over. In the time we had been there, Seventh Ave had gone from a street of three elderly ladies and bach owners to a fourteen-house street owned by a high court judge, the crown solicitor, a district judge, two lawyers, the managing director of a major company, and a convicted conman – the rest holiday weekenders. How times change.

Floor Shows from the Pub Window

*B*efore the Onetangi Pub opened in late September 1959, one hardly ever saw a pleasure craft in the bay. The sandy bottom was considered too dangerous to anchor on. At this stage yachts and launches were becoming more sophisticated with depth sounders, radio and modern gadgets. The lure of the pub saw the arrival of many craft on summer Saturdays.

Patrons in the public bar had a great view out the front windows at the weekly 'floor shows.' Dingies from the anchored craft either canning out on their way in, or going out as they battled the waves, usually very small waves. In each case a loud cheer would go up.

Local, Ned Davis, told me, every Sunday morning he would walk the beach from the toilet block area to the eastern end, on the look out for full bottles of beer that had been lost overboard to wash up on the overnight incoming tides. The labels had usually washed off, but as he said, 'Beggars can't be fussy when free beer was readily available.'

During those early days there were three drownings. On the first Labour Weekend Saturday the pub was opened and a young guy in his twenties went into the bar at 9am on his own to drink whisky with beer chasers. Around lunchtime he walked along the beach to the pohutukawa tree (the Hanging Tree) to go for a swim. It's not known whether he drowned, or the cold water reacted to his obviously warm whiskey-fed body to give him a heart attack.

The next drowning was the following year. A guy was stepping out of a dinghy on to a launch carrying a dozen carton of beer, he slipped, went straight to the bottom – still holding the beer. By the time his mates got him to the surface he was gone.

In the later 1960s, one New Year's Day, a visiting Scotsman on a launch went scuba diving with his mates in the early afternoon. He was the master of his own destiny, as after a few more drinks pre-lunch, he should never have gone in the water. After time had elapsed and he hadn't surfaced, the helicopter was called. It hovered for an hour before one of the rescue boats located the body. It was too late of course. There haven't been any drownings since, to my knowledge.

One Saturday walking along the Strand towards the pub, I noticed a twenty-two foot yellow yacht had slipped its anchor and was riding on top of a wave. I cut across the hotel lawn to the then beer garden, I yelled out, 'If anyone owns a yellow yacht that's out in front of the pub, you better get to it, as its riding the waves.' A guy got up and slowly sauntered over to me. He took one look and shouted to his mates, all four took off for the beach. By the time I got to the bar, they had roped in their wandering boat.

Over the years I've seen many incidents, mostly stupid but one always gives me a light. One Thursday afternoon, a New Zealand navy Fairmile came into the bay to anchor over at Woodlands. eight sailors and Wrens piled into a navy double-ended cutter to row over to the pub. They straightened up to row in surf-boat style. However, the guy on the rear oar lost control and over she went.

As the wet sailors entered the bar they were greeted by an almighty cheer from the patrons. One of the wrens went up the bar to say the inevitable words, 'Do you take wet money?' Another cheer went up.

One Thursday afternoon, the usual crowd, plus women at the usual time, at the usual leaner, were looking out to sea. When a forty foot trimaran came sailing towards the bar. I thought he was too close. I was assured by experienced yachties, including one frequent sailor in the Auckland-Fiji yacht Race, that they were ok. The tri suddenly shuddered to a halt, stranded on the bottom. I couldn't help myself. In a loud voice I said, 'Yeah I know nuthin', but I knew he was too bloody close.'

Back when 10 o'clock closing first came in, a well-known local leased a fishing boat from one of the big Auckland companies and anchored in the bay. However, after a long session in the pub, he went home to Surfdale. He returned the next morning nice and early to find the boat up on the beach. Luckily, it was not damaged. At the high tide, with local help he returned the boat to the sea. His bosses never knew.

Over the years there have been some excellent barmen and barmaids, too many to mention in one story. There were also some shockers. One temporary barman I had to admonish. One Saturday in the six o'clock closing days, I told him he was supposed to be serving me, as he kept filling his own glass to drink the publican's profits.

One barman, a gay guy, was quite a character. I got to know him well. In those early days of retirement, I rode a Roadster bike, one gear and had a beer crate tied onto my back carrier. Every Thursday morning, I rode over to the Ostend Four-Square. Coming back along the Onetangi Straight was hard work, riding into the usual northerly breeze.

During Summer I wore shorts and the barman would pass me on his way to work. When I went to the pub, he would smile at me and say 'Ooh, I saw a lovely pair of legs today.' One afternoon two guys dressed in Army camouflaged fatigues were standing on the sea side of the road. The barman came mincing over to our leaner, he said, 'Look at them, a couple of f#$%*&* queers, then overdid the mincing on his way back to the bar. It brought the house down.

Another day two local girls in their early twenties got into a fight. They went outside onto the road and got stuck in. Punches, scratching and hair pulling. Of course we had ringside seats and were cheering them on. The friendly barmen went out, got between them, then ordered them to return to the bar. Probably if any of us spectators had gone out to split them up, they would've taken to us.

Thursday 4pm to 6pm was 'Happy hour.' It was also 'tradies night out.' It was great if you needed a tradie you could get one. Usually, the job was done the following Thursday when you had a beer with him and paid him cash of course. I got a lot of jobs done that way.

The McGinty's Era

When we moved to Seventh Ave in 1980, a hundred yards in front of us was McGinty's Lodge run by race caller and Auctioneer Keith Haub, and his wife, Joy. McGinty's was a popular place named after a racehorse the Haubs had owned and who won several big races.

On summer Sundays the grass area in front of the lodge would be full of drinkers, there to hear the Gypsy Pickers perform. Keith usually got the day moving by rendering his favourite auctioneer song. Anyone could up and play and sing.

Around this time, they had obtained a TAB license, besides being busy with the usual bettors, several Saturdays they ran a punter's club. Patrons put ten dollars in, then Keith and others placed bets, all winnings went into the pool, with the winnings paid out at the end of the day.

One very memorable Saturday, we had quite a bit of luck, coming up to the last race the stake was about $3,000, meaning a possible $100 pay out each. It was agreed we would be on a horse that was owned by the bach owner next to McGinty's called Peter Buffalora.

Keith stunned the patrons when he yelled, 'Why don't we put the lot on to win.' There was silence. I was quite happy to do so. We had had a good day and were on a good run. You could tell most weren't willing, they were worried we would lose the lot.

It was decided to bet a hundred bucks to win and fifty bucks to place. The horse duly won and everyone went home happy. The next day I saw Keith at Eddie's Store collecting the Sunday paper. I said to him, 'You would've put the lot on wouldn't you, I would've backed you up.' He had said he was, 'just joking,' when he had made the original announcement. 'But too right I would,' he said with a big smile.

The TAB at McGinty's was lucky for me. I won more money out of that TAB than any other. Whenever I won big and told Joy how I'd pick the winners, Joy would say to Keith, 'You think you can pick winners but listen to Norm's theory.'

One Easter I had done a small job for a guy who gave me fifty bucks. I was normally a two dollar each way bettor, or no more than five dollars each way, but I decided to put the whole fifty on the nose in my selection for the Easter Handicap at Ellerslie. I checked the Herald, my lucky horoscope number was seven, colour blue. My pick was Sirstazi, number seven, jockey's colours, blue and white.

We had a crowd at the bach. I asked all the ladies, what number they wanted, then put one dollar each way on for them. Our friend from Glen Eden, Heather, while selecting her numbers remarked, 'Here's one for you, Norm, Bourbon Boy.' I hadn't told her my pick. It was a secret to the end. I took advice and quinnelled my two picks for two dollars.

Everyone was stacked around the TV. Off they went. Everyone was talking. They came round the bend, into the straight; my horse went to the outside. 'Quiet,' I boomed out. Sirstazi hit the lead and stayed there – I yelled, 'I've just won the most money ever.' Lynne of course thought I may have put ten bucks on. I held up a foolscap page with $1814 on it. Heather said Bourbon Boy had gotten second, the Quinella. I changed the figure to $2,245. What a night we had.

That was a good year. Later, I won $3000 on a three-dollar trifecta. On New Year's Eve, there was only Lynne, me, and Heather at the bach. I never bet on the trots but decided to have a bet on the Auckland Trotting Cup. I did the usual, asked the two what number they wanted. Lynne said ten. I told her I would take a three-dollar trifecta for her with our week's lucky number. Ten won, Lynne won $2000. My winnings went towards a 5,000-gallon concrete tank. Lynne purchased a painting. The TAB didn't get any of our winnings back. It was a good year for a Saturday-only, small-time bettor.

McGinty's was originally called Spray's Edge. Back in the 1940s it was a private hotel. Our Point Chev neighbour and his family went there every Christmas holidays for many years. There was Danny and Morrie, very good chefs, and entertainers. Their specialty was midweek packages for pensioners. They loved it. Then there was the infamous Barbara Doyle. She tried to get a casino there but was turned down by the authorities. This was long before the Sky Tower came on the scene. Barbara also owned a pub in Thames where she ran 'Murder weekends,' guests played parts, then had to guess who the murderer was.

Sadly, McGinty's came to an end when Keith and Joy split up. Keith went back to the city. Joy has remained an Onetangi resident and we love chatting to her when we meet. McGinty's was sold to a Hawkes Bay Developer. While waiting for plans to be drawn up, and for resource management approval, McGinty's was leased by a group of young people. They painted the front with bright colours and called it 'Onetangi Yacht Club.'

On Friday evenings they ran a 'beer fest' night, catering for city types who would book a ticket for boat to Matiatia, then bus to the venue, then return the same night. The buses would arrive at 7pm, leaving around 11pm to catch the last boat to the city.

The first song would be 'Roll out the Barrel.' At the finish it was 'Old Lang Syne.' I didn't mind as the music was good. There was no boom boom from a loud base and the night was over before midnight. However, several of the locals were not so happy and made complaints. The Yacht Club only had a short life as the building was demolished and the developer moved in.

The Easter I won the money we had a full house at the bach. Besides our usual lot, Denny, a Maori lad our son's age, who had always been a good friend, came with two English girls. Denny played the guitar and sang; he was a good entertainer, and had busked his way around England, and performed in cave-type bars on Gibraltar. He had also crewed on flash boats on the Mediterranean. Denny had taught his 'English Roses' to harmonise. On the Saturday night, Lynne's sister, Anne, husband, and friends, Jim and Ethel, turned up. We had a good sing song and taped it. Next morning, we played the tape. The first part was good enough to play on a radio station. The flip side was a shocker as the voices got impaired by the liquor intake. Denny and I had done a rendition of the 'Banana Boat Song' – he sang, and I did the background 'Day-O's.'

On Sunday afternoon it was off to McGinty's. Keith knew Denny and after doing his opening 'auctioneer,' Keith called up Denny who performed, then he called the girls up, they were good. Next, he said on the mike, 'C'mon Norm let's do the 'Banana Boat.' No bloody way was I going to perform (sober) before that crowd.

Denny came back about ten years later. He couldn't get over the change – fast boats, lots of cars, development of Oneroa, Surfdale and Ostend, and a supermarket. He had brought a bag with meat and perishables like we had to in those earlier years.

That was some twenty years ago. He would certainly be surprised if he returned. Sadly, we have lost contact as we were both very fond of Denny. We miss his big smile and laugh.

For four months a seagull adopted me to become my pet. I often put breadcrumbs out on the terrace. One day one of them took over and shooed the rest of them away. From then on when I pulled my curtains back at 8am and looked down towards the lamppost in front of McGinty's there would be Sid, perched waiting. Then he was off on a bee line to my terrace.

If I slept in, I would hear him screeching outside my bedroom window, telling me to get up to get his breakfast. If another seagull came near him, he would attack them. Gradually, I enticed him on to the wide windowsill to be an arms-length away. Then one morning he wasn't on the lamppost. I never saw him again. Although one day several months later a seagull circled several times, then landed on the terrace rail. I thought it might be Sid, returning to check on me.

Finally, the McGinty's era came to an end. The bulldozers

Norm's pet seagull, Sid, 1993

moved in, the building was demolished, and construction of the Sands commenced. Over a year or so, the building rose skywards, fortunately for us it never became a problem. We looked right over the top, our view was not impaired in any way.

Like all buildings constructed at that time it was left with the leaky home syndrome. For several years there were builders working on the roof. I was always amazed during construction to see painters and plasterers arrive from town at 5pm, then work during the night. I know both trades cannot work when conditions get too cold – unless they had heaters to keep the rooms warm, they could have had problems. Most units were not built with terraces, they took up too much space. The planned restaurant and bar got deleted by local 'sometime weekenders' who had objected. For us, life went on.

Other Characters

*O*ur neighbours, across the road at Seventh Ave were the Trigg Family. Their parents, Noel and Mary, were also hosts at Prince Arthur Hotel and formerly of the City Hotel, purchased the property during the 1940s. It had been one of the original Onetangi properties. Lynne and I never met Noel or Mary. But we did get to know the rest of the family over holiday times. There were their older daughter, Pat, and husband, George Fisher, sisters, Gail and Morrie, and the younger brother, Barry. Barry was in residence when I retired, then Pat and George took over in their retirement in the mid-1990s. Later, they moved to the Waiheke Retirement Village where George passed away.

Barry was two years older than me. He was an alcoholic and never denied it. He even told stories against himself. Pat described him as a 'happy drunk' and some of his adventures were legendary. His main claim to fame was that he went over the bank on the Strand in his car with his mate, Tony. Many pub patrons also achieved that distinction, but Barry also did it on a pushbike – the only one to do it two different ways.

One Easter Sunday morning, after the old boys meeting at the sports club, we spotted Barry driving home along the Strand. He was obviously unaware of the police car behind him. Barry parked in the road behind the house. He got out, then slowly slid along the side to the rear to finish up leaning on the boot.

By this time the cop was standing beside him, he asked the usual question, 'Have you been drinking Sir?' According to Barry, he replied, 'Only had a couple, officer. I've been to a meeting at the sports club.' The police officer was well aware it was a social meeting, not one to discuss club business. George and Morrie who were there for the holiday weekend had to come out and assist Barry down the stairs to the house. Barry lost his license and bought a bike. Barry had the habit of riding the bike to the pub. Being incapable of riding it home he would ask me. No problem. I would ride it to his house, place it by the back door then head off up the stairs, and across the road to my place.

One Saturday the usual happened but Barry couldn't get a lift home, so he walked. Once again, we spotted him coming along the Strand, he turned into Seventh Ave, just past the steps to Sea View Road, he staggered, then fell down the grassy bank. His two brothers in law went down, got him up on to the road to help him home.

When Barry was in residence and living on his own, he had frequent mid-week visitors. Fred Trout was one. There was also a group of hard-shot girls, plus others. One day one of his mates, another alcoholic, was painting the coves twenty feet up a ladder. I was waiting for the crash, but he clambered down rather wobbly just before lunch, leaving the paint tin and brush beside the ladder, then went to the pub. He never came back, leaving Barry to do the clean up.

Barry had married and had two sons, Johnny and Darci. He spent quite a few years in Port Villa as the skipper of a luxury yacht catering to tourists. As an apprentice carpenter, he had lost three fingers. He would tell the tourists that he lost them fighting off a shark. They believed him. He told me it was a great job. After returning to the berth at the yacht club, he would clean up, then join them at the bar, great, they had plenty of money and always shouted.

For a short time, Barry had a girlfriend, she was a local and lived, handily, close by. She was a bit strange and was known to be affected by the full moon. One Sunday morning she called on Barry. For some reason he didn't want to see her so he locked the back door. Beside the back door were several crates of empty bottles. The upset girl proceeded to take the empties out of the crate and throw them through the kitchen windows, smashing most of them.

She went around to the front of the house to try and put one through the massive window in the lounge. Luckily, she was unable to get one high enough to smash it. By then she had had enough and went home. We later heard that her parents took her away from the island. Maybe too many bad influences in her life. Lynne went down and helped clean up. She said there was glass everywhere.

Barry led a colourful life. Triggy, as he was mostly known by, sailed in several Auckland Suva Yacht races with his mate Tony Jurd. He also delivered yachts around the Pacific and had several enterprises on the island. He died aged seventy-two, a real Waiheke character.

Barry's son Darci came back to Waiheke from Australia a few years before his dad died. I got to know Darci very well. A chip off the old block, Darci loved his beer. He had a serious medical condition and took a bucket load of pills. Often hospitalized, he would walk out, then the authorities would come looking for him.

Like his dad, he loved a good story, and was happy to tell stories about himself. He told me of his time in Vanuatu when he was about six. He also told me about how when he was the age of fifteen, he would stay at the house when Noel and Mavis were there. He and his mates would raid the booze cabinet. They would then come across the road to drink in the reserve next door to my place.

I surprised him when I said, 'So that was you who left the bottles on my section. I took a wheelbarrow full to the bin at the bottom of seventh Ave. Darci was great mates with well know Rocky Bay artist, Mike Morgan, and local legend, Jimmy Hodgetts. Sadly, Darci passed away before he made fifty.

In the late fifties there was a family in Sixth Ave, Onetangi, called Bear. The father's name was Jim but he was better known as 'Grizzly.' He spoke with a deep raspy voice and suited the name. Wife, Olive, son, Teddy, who was a rather large lad, I'm told he was teased badly at School, plus cat, 'Polar.'

One Easter weekend after a heavy drinking session with several locals, their house burned down to the ground. Doctor Montgomery, a pipe smoking heavy drinker died in the fire. He was an elderly guy at the time and was sleeping on the sofa. The allegations surfaced that he dropped his still burning pipe that started the fire. Jim stayed on the island after, but Olive went to live in town.

Over the years, I've had quite a few Maori friends on the island. In 1960 when I ran off the rails and Eddie and I would head to the boozer for the early morning session, there were several early starters. Jimmy Ngapo and his younger brother, Henry, were always there in the corner of the bar, next to the door that led into the lounge.

Henry was possibly the biggest man on the island. He was built like a rugby union prop forward but had one leg cut off above the knee. His crutches were made from tea-tree wood. He would always have the corner position so he could lean against the bag. Henry would always still be there when we went home to lunch. It appears that if he stayed too long and got too boozed, he got aggressive. Finally, they barred him. He went to live in the Thames area, and we never saw him again.

Jimmy Ngapo was tall and thin and was the island fishing inspector. His work included working on the oyster boat, the Tio. Jimmy had served overseas with the Maori Battalion and was good army mates with our Glen Eden neighbour, Dick Williams. Several times on a Saturday night, Eddie and I finished up at Ngapo's for a boozy night. I got to know his wife Minnie very well, a lovely lady. Lynne also got to know her. Whenever we met, Minnie would always ask after Keith and Sarndra by name. Jimmy died several years before Minnie.

The day before Minnie died, Lynne and I had moved to the village. I was surprised to see the Tio come into Anzac Bay. Knowing Minnie was in the last throws of her life, I thought it was an omen. I told their daughter Kathryn of the coincidence. The Tio looked very dilapidated and there appeared to be a guy staying on board, gradually it sank. Several months later the harbour board removed it to tow it to its grave.

When the pub first opened, a guy named Kingi Stevens was a Saturday barman, he was my age, a big lad, immaculately dressed in black trousers and shoes, white shirt, black bow tie, brown oval face with beautiful white teeth, dark eyes, and black cropped hair. He was always smiling. We got on well.

On Saturday afternoons when I arrived, he would great me with, 'Hi Stephens with a ph.' I would reply, 'How did a Maori like you get a name like Stevens.' During the week he would revert to his full-time job as a bus driver. Kingi would wear a pair of black shorts, grey singlet, and bare feet. He also drove the school bus. He was eventually told to wear more appropriate clothes. Kingi didn't and the bus company suspended him. The school kids then threatened to go on strike as they all loved him. Kingi loved singing and would get all the kids singing along. The kids won the day and Kingi was restored.

Most Saturdays in the afternoon when he had 'one over the eight,' Graham Tawhai would start singing. Most Maoris I've met could sing, but not Graham, like me, he was 'flat.' He would start usually looking straight down at the bar, sliding along it as he sang. My mate Eddie always said, 'Can you sing far away, like over at Rooster Point?' I knew his sons Jerry and Graeme well.

In the nineties I met a part Maori guy called 'Mouldy' or Michael Mulholland. My first encounter with him was in the lounge bar at the pub. It was being used because the bar area was being refurbished after a fire. Mouldy was a hard angry man. He had been a gang member, been in goal and known to dabble in drugs. There was a radio on the bar. Mouldy turned it up loud, then walked back towards his table.

As he got level with me, I said, 'Oi, we don't want to listen to that, we came for a quiet beer.' To my surprise he went back to turn it off. We became great mates after that. Twice he turned up unannounced at the bach. When we were concreting the front path, he took over the mixer. He Also helped with the barbeque on my sixtieth birthday. Later he split with his partner to go to Wellington. He was stabbed to death on Taita Street, where he lived, on twentieth of September 2012 over a drug deal. He was buried in his TeTeko hometown. Two men were convicted of his murder.

In Hobson Terrace we had an Irish neighbour, Jimmy Flynn. He grew his own marijuana and smoked it. When he got high he would go out on his terrace to play his fiddle and dance in the nude. Most people couldn't see him as he was on the high side of the road, the back surrounded by pine trees. However, my back neighbour in Trig Hill Road had a bird's eye view.

When the pub first allowed women into the bar, the first two were an older woman and a local girl, Rosanne (probably underage). Boy, could they swear, make a miner blush. 'Rosie' as she was better known was quite a hard drinker. She had green eyes and could look right through you. I think she had had a hard life. She had a son. This caused much speculation among the pub patrons. No one knew to my knowledge who the father was. Like many I had my suspicions, but would certainly not ask her. No doubt she would have given me a biff.

Over the years I got to know Rosie. In the ninties she married Ray, possibly the best decision she ever made. For several years she was a barmaid and ran the TAB at the pub. On Melbourne Cup Day I helped out, filling cards in for the 'oldies' and giving advice on how to bet and doing general customer liaison. It was a good day for me – free beer, and a pie for lunch. Lynne got to meet Rosie and liked her. Sadly, on a trip out to Greenland Hospital for me, Ray was on the bus. Rosie was in Auckland Hospital. They had discovered a tumour on the brain. It was terminal. She died soon after. Very sad, it was the best time of her life. Yes, Waiheke has had many characters.

Memories

We all share the same types of memories – our first day at school, our first day at work, and our first girlfriend (or boyfriend). I had my first girlfriend when I was eighteen, a lovely girl, we had been in the same class at Pasadena Intermediate, but it didn't last long. I wasn't ready to go steady, tennis and footy were more fun.

My first car was a 1937 Morris 8. It cost £180 (about six month's pay) and I got it for my nineteenth birthday. My first overseas trip was as an Auckland under twenty-one rugby league rep to NSW. We sailed over on the *Wanganui*. It took four days at sea, we came home by Teal to Whenuapai. Of course there was my engagement, marriage, first home, children, each followed by many other events, all accomplished with a great array of photos.

Many events and disasters are often remembered by where you were at the time, or by a birthday. My longest, fondest memory is of my ninth birthday, fifteenth of August 1945. My mum was in Auckland Hospital having knee cartilage removed, three weeks operation and recovery in those days. I had the same operation forty years later. It took three hours, in and out, and three days recovery. Now it's even quicker. I had gone to stay with Cousin David, who was the same age, plus the same grade. The day was a Thursday and I was attending his Three Kings Primary School all week. After lunch we played footie on the school field. At the assembly bell, we all lined up on the square in front of the school's steps. The headmaster came out and announced, 'I have some good news. The war has ended. You can all go home. Don't come tomorrow, Friday. Remember school holidays start Monday. Now get your bags and all go straight home.' The school was cleared in ten minutes. I Remember mothers didn't work in those days and all kids walked to school. I must have told this story tons of times. I could tell you I wore black shorts and a grey shirt and bare feet. Typical of the day. We went home to tell my Aunty Grace it was VJ Day. Like many mothers, she was unaware until we turned up.

My good mate in my teen years was Neil Fox. He worked as an apprentice grocer in his grandfather Dave's 'Invincible Grocery' on Point Chev Road. Every Friday I would go to the shop at 8.30pm, when Neil knocked off. We would go up to Hall's Corner, the main shopping centre that included the Ambassador Movie Theatre, buy an ice-cream, then walk down one side of Point Chev Road to the beach, then back up the other side, discussing tennis or rugby league, whatever we were playing the next day.

On Christmas Eve in 1953, we decided to call in to the shop, knowing Dave and his mate Charlie would be listening to the broadcast from South Africa of the cricket test with New Zealand. Instead of the score we got the bad news of the Tangiwhai disaster, with many deaths and the recovery of bodies in carriages and the dark river. The bridge had collapsed with the weight of the train and the foundations had been weakened by the massive rush of water off the mountain.

In 1986 Lynne and I were on the Greek island of Kalymanos, where we spent ten of the best days of our lives. One late afternoon as we arrived back to our *pensione*, the two Swedish boys who were also staying in the room next to us greeted us with the news of the Chernobyl Nuclear explosion. There was major concern throughout Europe that the fallout would reach Greece. Athen's food markets were cleared of all supplies. As we travelled north towards England, we were to see many 'beware' signs as well as sheep with green markings on them.

My absolute worst memory was when I was eight years old. My sister Marion, who was four, nearly drowned. We lived in Meola Road, Point Chev. At that stage, the road only ran as far as Meola Creek. There was a bridge at the end leading towards Westmere. I, two other boys my age, and an older boy, John Calder, with Marion tagging along, went there one morning.

All the boys were facing upstream, watching sticks take speed up the creek. As it was a full tide the water was funnelling as it went under the bridge at its narrowest point. Somehow Marion had got herself on to the top rung of the bridge. She then slipped off and went under the bridge, into the torrent.

Our first sighting was seeing a floppy hat, bobbling along with Marion tied tightly to it. Her face would disappear then bob up again. None of us boys could swim. The other three took off up the path. It was mid-afternoon and wartime. Very luckily John's father who was in the Air Force was at that moment coming out of the gate on his way to the base, and was only fifty yards away.

Mr. Calder raced down the track, shedding his uniform and shoes as he came. Down to his underwear, he dived in to bring Marion back to the bridge area where I was stuck to the spot unable to help in any way. Mr. Calder carried Marion to our home 300 yards away. I had recovered and ran ahead to tell Mum.

Not surprisingly, Marion never remembered the incident, and Mum never told her. It was not until sixty years later when I wrote the family history that Marion read the story. A few years later I introduced John to Marion at a Point Chev reunion. Marion thanked him and his late father for their efforts on that day – I have never forgotten it.

I've had my fair share of accidents over the years. I think I've used up my nine lives. My first accident was when I was five, flying down a steep hill, hitting the curb and flying over the handlebars of my trike. I had a granny smith apple in my mouth. It was still there when I stood up.

When I was eight, I was helping two older boys to build a hut on the Westmere side of Meola Reef. I slipped, fell onto a sharp rock, and cut my head open. I took off for home, screaming all the way. The two older boys couldn't catch me. Mum reckoned she heard me 200 yards from home.

When I was twelve I got concussion while playing in a school rugby game. I was in hospital for a week. At ninteen I was the driver in a car accident, no injuries, just a shake up and a fine, my fault. A year later, it was the roll over in a van accident on Waiheke, where I received a broken collarbone.

At twenty-eight, with Lynne eight months pregnant with Sarndra, I had what could've been a very serious work accident. I was on the machine at Stahlton, pre-stressing the steel rods, when one snapped and went through the thigh muscle between the knee and the hip. I had 185 feet of steel rod in one side of my leg, with eighteen inches protruding out the other.

I yelled, 'Quick, someone come here.' The first guy into the shed was a Samoan, poor Ernie, he took one look, turned grey and ran up and down on the spot. Others arrived, plus the ambulance. They had to cut the long 185 feet end as close to my leg as possible. At the hospital they were all amazed. I was sitting up looking like an Indian with an arrow through his leg. They put me out, pulled the rod through, dressed the injury, then the ambulance took me home to Glen Eden. When Sarndra was born they put her blonder hair down to the incident. I was lucky, a few inches up or down and it could've shattered the knee or hip.

I badly hurt my knee in the latter years of my rugby league career. It gave me problems during the years. In 2011 I needed a full right knee replacement. Then there were the episodes of the two trees falling. The second one nearly wiped Lynne and I out completely.

In 2016 Lynne and I went on our last cruise – thirty-five days. At the furthermost point north of Auckland, I had a heart attack. I was worried I would be offloaded, flown to Honolulu, then back to Auckland. Luckily, they let me stay on the ship to complete the trip home. We docked on Wednesday thirteenth of May. At Lunchtime on Friday the Fifteenth I was choppered to Auckland Hospital.

It took ten days for the hospital to agree I could be operated on. I then had a four-way heart bypass, and four days in intensive care, then to the ward, thankfully, a single room. The first three nights I had hallucinations. Then I had complications, a serious laceration to my leg, which took till Christmas to heal. I also had a very serious ulcer under my tongue. The surgeon told me I was lucky the infection didn't go to my brain, as it would've been fatal. I was in hospital a total of eight weeks before I was released. Several months later I was back for a week due to two large leg ulcers. The tongue has never recovered.

Over the years I've had several back problems, due to car crashes, footie or heavy lifting jobs. In late 2016, I had a bad back spasm. At that stage, my lower vertebrae were fractured. It has never improved. Slowly my movements have also been hindered by balance problems to the extent I can hardly walk. I've gone from walking stick to wheelie, to motorized scooter. I can no longer drive due to eye problems. Luckily, I have Lynne to provide me with full time care. I would be lost without her, probably be in a rest home.

It has not been all doom and gloom. I have great memories, most dealing with sport. We have a loving family and at eighty-five I've surpassed in age all my forebears.

I've lived through some interesting times. Born during the Depression, primary school during World War Two, our school ground dug into trenches. We wore a camphor bag around our necks with a cork to put between our teeth, plus two pieces of cotton wool in case of a bomb blast. Intermediate school was the polio epidemic, Seddon Tech, the Korean conflict. I lived through the atomic bomb and the nuclear age, man on the moon, and too many floods and earthquakes. There was also the Mosque Massacre when a deranged Aussie killed fifty-one people. He should've been hanged, he's no bloody use to anyone, or sent back to Mozzieland as a reverse 501. I'm sure someone there would love to become infamous for slowly strangling him to death.

Finally, I remember the evening I went with cousins, Terry and David, to the scout den in Kingsland. It was my only time, but I did learn the scouts' motto; 'be prepared.' I've used it extensively ever since. As a teenager I always carried a bottle opener and a pack of cards in my weekend bag. You would be amazed the number of times I was the only one with both. Lynne and I, when travelling, swapped the bottle opener for a Swiss Army knife - just have to remember to take it out of hand luggage before boarding airplanes.

Now in and out of old age we have our hospital bag handy as advised. We have both had to use it. Now as we get ready for our last voyage, we have arranged our wills, power of attorney and told our family what to do with chattels etc. We have had our ash caskets built and signwriting (one line to be filled) these are photographed on the last page. We will be interred in the same plot at Waiheke cemetery.

For the rest of the time, we will live it up.

Yeah right!

The Last Word

As I write the last story of my Waiheke Tales, I must mention two prominent New Zealand self-made men who are both known worldwide. They both have a special love for our beautiful Waiheke Island.

One Lynne and I have known for over fifty years. The other I have only met briefly on two occasions, many years apart. The former is the 'Mad Butcher,' Sir Peter Leitch and his lovely wife, Janice. We first met them when they stayed with the Cowley family on Eden Terrace. Our bach was sixty yards away on Hobson Terrace.

Peter and I shared a love of rugby league, the Kiwis, then later the inconsistent Warriors. At this stage Peter had his first butcher shop and sponsored the local Mangere East Club. From 1976-8 I coached the Glenora premier team and was known in the Auckland rugby league scene.

In 1980, we shifted to the western end. A year later Peter and Janice purchased a property on the Strand, about a hundred yards as the crow flies from our new abode. Peter had a morning radio show to promote his wares, as well as any any sporting event going. One morning over the Christmas holiday season, Peter was chatting about Onetangi and he mentioned 'Norm Stephens and his family have an old tin shed up on the hill from their holiday home.'

I didn't hear the show, but when I walked into the pub at 4pm, many of the patrons had. That was Peter, one of his jokes I was reminded about many times with the remark, 'How's the tin shed, Norm?' Peter was a hard worker and built up a chain of shops around the country. He was always prepared and still supports many sports in a number of ways. He was a New Zealand rugby league manager when we won the World Cup.

The man I met briefly when he was about fourteen was Bruce Plested of Mainfreight fame. It was a Saturday during the Christmas holidays of 1960. Eddie and I had caught an early bus out of Onetangi to go to the island's first TAB, then in Oneroa, to place a bet. On the bus on the way back as we approached the green shed on the border of Ostend and Palm Beach, Eddie said, 'C'mon get off here.'

When we got off, he said he knew a guy who had a place along the road towards Palm Beach. We hadn't walked far when we heard a voice. 'You guys looking for me?' It was Leo Vaile in his front garden digging a hole. It was about 11am. He said, 'Time for a brew, you guys must've walked a long way.' Seeing Eddie and knowing he lived in Onetangi, he had surmised we had walked from there. We put him right.

He led the way up to the bach, introduced us to his wife, Doris. We went to the front of the house to the covered veranda and bunkroom. Over the years we had more sessions. We drank Leo's Lucious Liquor or Vaile's Viscous Vintage. He said he left his bad brews for unwanted visitors.

The brew was made the old way, in an old washing machine bowl, with a sack over the top and with hops. As we finished a carton which he pulled out from under a wire-wove-bed-frame that had no legs, he would replace it with another carton.

Their daughter Lorraine, who would've been in her late teens, was deaf. She came out and pointed her finger at each one of us, put her thumb and forefinger to her nose, then made a sign of pulling the chain, then laughed. Sadly, Lorraine died at an early age.

We listened to the radio broadcast of the Auckland - Canterbury Cricket game and the races (we didn't win). About 4pm four young teenage boys who had been at the beach all day came in. They were the Vaile's boys, Ken and Ray, plus Arch Hill neighbours, Carl and Bruce Plested. Leo introduced us to the boys. We were obviously in their room and they went off to play cards.

At 6pm as the Cricket finished, I suggested to Eddie it was time to go. A couple of the boys went down the road to get the local taxi guy to pick us up to take us home. What a day. Meeting the Vaile family and the boys. It would be the first of many days with the Vailes. I didn't meet Bruce Plested again until fifty years later.

All four boys went on to buy properties near the Vaile's Palm Beach homestead, a happy place for them as they enjoyed their boyhood holidays there. As Ken and Ray got older, I was to enjoy many a beer with them and their dad on summer Saturdays in the Onetangi boozer.

Bruce started up the Mainfreight business and it has become a worldwide empire. An obvious hard worker, he reminds me very much of my old Ceramco boss, the late Sir Tom Clark, who was known, as a young guy, to sleep near the kilns at the Amalgamated Brick and Pipe Co in the early stages of the company, long before it joined up with the other family company, Crown Lynn Potteries to became Ceramco.

One Saturday I met up with Leo in the pub. I hadn't seen him for a while. He was quite excited. He told me how Bruce had paid for him and Doris to go on holiday to Doris's birthplace in Newcastle, England as repayment for all his happy days at Palm Beach with their family.

Later Bruce purchased Pie Melon Bay. He has planted many native trees there. His farm manager, Joe Muir, lent me a book that is about the Bay property and the growth of Mainfreight, *Rorohara*, a very interesting story. Lately, Bruce purchased the Carey's Bay property that joins up with Pie Melon Bay, covering that whole peninsular. He has plans for many more native trees to be planted.

Over the years I've had many walks with my mate Eddie Smith over this area. Eddie was caretaker at Carey's for several years. One day we and Lynne walked up to Rooster Point where they are several graves, over a hundred years old, of the Carey family. Marge

Le Franchi, the former Onetangi Pub owner was a Carey.

The only other time I saw and spoke briefly with Bruce Plested was as Doris Vail's funeral, a lovely lady. For me, although I've only met him twice, I feel I've known him all my life.

Lastly there are two Onetangi couples we have got to know well over the past thirty years. Whenever I meet up with Grunter and Rose, it is always a race to see who can produce the first joke. Some years ago, Grunter had a medical mishap that needed a liver transplant. Grunter, a hard drinker was told by his surgeon he could never touch alcohol again in his life.

The surgeon informed him it would take six months to clear his system even before an operation could be performed. He also told him, if he drank after the op, he would never get another replacement. Most of his mates doubted he could adhere to the 'no drink' doctrine. Grunter, a heavy machine operator also had to give up his job. I admire him for taking the advice. He took on embroidery, starting his own company, mainly embroidering sportswear. It is magic to see him working his machine.

The other couple are Rob and Dulcie and their girls. They lived not far from us on Seaview Road. The family delivered *the Marketplace* paper every Wednesday for most of the years we were in Seventh Ave. We could always expect a 'Hi Norm or Lynne' by whichever family member was on delivery duty. Dulcie was also our postie.

Once a month on a Thursday, Dulcie and her postie work mate Sally, would have a 'girls' night out'. Usually, I would be leaving the pub when they walked in. Now and again, around 10pm on their way home, I would hear a car stop, two doors open, then close. A few moments later a knock on the door. They loved my home brew.

After a couple of beers, Dulcie would ring Rob, he would walk down, have a beer then drive them home. Grunter and Rose, Rob, Dulcie and 'young' Dulcie all attended my sixtieth birthday party at Onetangi along with other locals to make it a night to remember.

I also had a family sixtieth at Newmarket's Bodrum Turkish restaurant. Yes, I did the belly dance when challenged in the traditional manner. My bare belly was not quite as graceful as the dancer, but there was plenty of it to show off.

Finally, the last word, which is a word, a very yuppy word that was first heard after the millennium had introduced us into the twenty-first century. A word that came at the time Nikki Kaye won the Auckland central seat for the first time for the National party at the 2006 election.

It was a stage where ordinary Waiheke homes were hitting the million-dollar mark. Rich listers were buying up large and the island was experiencing major changes. There was also a bar at Surfdale with the same name. It didn't last too long. I think the prices were too high.

That terrible word was 'Waihitian' the new way of calling people from Waiheke. At the time I wrote a letter to the Waiheke Marketplace (11 Jan 2002) pointing out that Waihekeans came from Waiheke and Waihitians came from Waihitia, wherever that was, somewhere in the Pacific, I guess. A few weeks ago, I was shocked and amazed to see that W. word rear its ugly head in a letter to the Gulf News. Please let us not go through that palaver again. I'm a *Waihekean* from Waiheke and proud of it.

Norm's Passion ~ Coaching Rugby League

It was inevitable I would be a 'Leaguey,' as when I was ready for 'footie' rugby league was the only winter code played in Point Chev. Recently when researching my family ancestry, I discovered my great, great, grandparents on my father's, mother's side were both born in the Lancashire town of Wigan, as were their twelve children.

Wigan was a founder member of the English rugby league and have always been my favourite British team. They have always been one of the top two sides. In their competitions, several New Zealand players and coaches have been involved in the 'Cherry and Whites.' In 1980 we watched the Kiwis play England at their ground.

I started playing in the seven-a-sides in 1946 aged nine for Point Chevalier, right through until 1970 when I was thirty-four as player-coach of the reserve grade. I played every schoolboy grade. Then five great years in the juniors. We had a very good team and won the competition every year. Coach for three of those years was Jack Wright, an ex-Point Chev senior captain. He was the best coach I ever had. I learned a lot from him. I made the under-nineteen reps in 1954 and was selected in the Auckland under twenty-one team that toured NSW for four unbeaten games in 1957.

From 1958 it was Point Chev seniors and reserves, including five years with Western United during the district scheme. In 1965 I was captain of the senior team, an honour for me that I was very proud of.

A neck injury during the following season ended my playing days. For the rest of the season, I coached club under-eighteen teams. In 1967 I coached the club reserve grade team, we made the grand final but lost, a big disappointment. The next two years we were average. In my last year, we had a slow start. I played the last thirteen games. We won the Bottom section championship. That was my last season at Point Chev, aged thirty-four.

We were living in Glen Eden at this stage. I coached my son Keith's Glenora schoolboy team from 1972 to 73. In 1974 to 75, I took over the Glenora under-nineteen team. We won the competition both years. The second year we lost half the team because of their age. The replacements did a grand job. In the following three years, eleven of these boys played premiers.

In 1976 I was selected over two ex-Kiwis to coach the Glenora premier team. Glenora covered a large area from Glen Eden, Oratia, New Lynn, Kelston and Henderson, bigger than many NZ towns. Also, Glenora was the biggest rugby league club in New Zealand. It was a big responsibility. For me, it was a dream come true. The main man. Coaching was a lot different then. I was sole coach, selector and trainer. Unlike today with the world of assistants, trainers, physios, even doctors. I had a manager, a masseur, and on game days, a gear steward.

That season we came from fourth to the grand final against minor premiers, Mt. Wellington. We led all the way but were overtaken in the last five minutes. We were shattered. We were the underdogs but missed out on a major upset. I still have bad dreams about that day.

In 1977 we made the top four and were beaten in the Roope Rooster final. After a slow start in 1978, I dropped several players to reserve grade and we improved over the season to win the Roope Rooster Comp over Mangere East 12 – 3. It was the club's first major victory in sixteen years. I wasn't wanted for 1979, some committee

**Glen Eden Rec Grounds 4 June 1978, Glenora 12 v Otahuhu 3,
a very satisfying victory**

men were unhappy with me for putting ex-All Black Joe Karam back to reserve grade in that early season player re-shuffle.

Over the seventies I had coached Auckland junior teams in fifteen unbeaten games including the under seventeen national title in 1980. I was selected as New Zealand Junior Kiwis coach for 1981 tour of Australia and the 1982 tour of Papua-New Guinea. In all, I coached the Juniors in seventeen games, the most of any coach.

I coached City Newton premier in 1983 and my old club Point Chev seniors in 1984. During my big OE with Lynne in 1986, I coached the Huddersfield team in a caretaker capacity after the team had lost eleven straight. We lost the first to top four, Swinton, then went to London where we beat Fulham in a mud heap. The first win in twelve games. The players whooped for joy as if they had won lotto. It was seventy-five pounds for a win (the average wage in Yorkshire) against fifteen pounds for a loss. We had decided to come back to New Zealand as Keith was getting married, plus my boss offered me my job back.

Over the years I was Auckland coaching director and on the New Zealand Rugby League coaching panel. When I came back, I decided to call rugby league quits. I'd had enough. More time for Waiheke.

I knew from my junior playing days I would be a coach. My ability to play all positions helped me. I loved coaching. it gave me a buzz to walk into the changing rooms at Carlaw Park, the smell of liniment, the adrenalin, the atmosphere, and afterwards the thrill of winning over the disappointment of losing, and the thrill of seeing your players go on to rep honours. Even now, some thirty plus years later I'm in touch with guys from my playing and coaching days.

Ah! Great memories. Great guys.

Travelling Together

$\mathcal{L}$ynne and I loved traveling. Fortunately, we travelled well together. Our usual method of planning for travel was to select our destination together. Then I would gather the necessary information, maps, or booklets regarding the area. In our travels through Greece and the Mediterranean we had a small booklet, shirt pocket size. It was invaluable. When traveling I wrote the diary and kept an eye on the costs. Lynne was the photographer.

Over our sixty years of married life, we visited over forty countries including many Pacific islands and much of the east coast of Australia. We have seen most of New Zealand by car, or rental including a three-week bus tour of the South Island. We have seen the five islands of the country. Travel has been by all modes, aeroplane, cruise liner, ship, launch, rail, bus, and car.

The highlight was our 1986 'World Walkabout' that included six weeks in the Greek islands, staying on eight islands, overnight and twice ten days. If there was one thing, I could do in my life was spend about seven months, early spring until late Autumn traveling light and island hopping the Mediterranean, visiting places we haven't yet been. Oh, to dream!

There is a misnomer when told not to wear insignia that tells where you come from. Go to any airport, train station, or bus park and stand outside. Doesn't matter whether you are in New Zealand

Wednesday Morning

NZ Herald 5/8/87

Backpacking freestyle

G ENERALLY, middle age is a time for people to watch television travel documentaries and dream of a world package tour in their retirement, or to listen to their children's travel tales of backpacking, living cheaply and getting to out-of-the-way places.

For many people past the age of 40, going anywhere without a detailed itinerary is just not done.

However, at 49 I and my wife of 25 years, Lynne (45) spent 10½ months backpacking through

dinner to prepare ourselves for the six to seven miles of walking we planned to do while exploring cities, islands and other places of interest. During our absence our son, Keith and daughter, Sarndrn, were to live in our house.

Before leaving, we prepaid our flight to Athens, including a two-day Singapore stopover, plus a six-day tour of Greece (a great way to get acclimatised to travel) and also a one-month Eurail pass. We did not arrange return fares as we had both left our jobs and were not sure how long we would be away.

cities of Hania and Rhodes. We also walked the famous Samaria Gorge trek on Crete.

Transport around the Greek islands was by ship or launch, and our 10 inter-island trips cost a total of $300. Finding the times of sailings was sometimes time-consuming, as it was necessary to check with the various shipping offices — on some islands there were two or three different agencies.

Accommodation was fairly easily obtained: people made offers as we disembarked. Most rooms were not sure how long we would be away.

TRAVEL

If, as the saying goes, life begins at 40, there is still plenty of time to visit some interesting places without a detailed itinerary, as NORM STEPHENS discovered during travels with his wife, Lynne.

Europe and the United Kingdom recently, going where the whim or the mood dictated, stopping longer in some places and changing our proposed itinerary as we felt necessary.

In the months before our departure we had spent hours poring over maps, travel brochures, Eurail timetables and any information we could obtain on the countries we planned to visit.

Compulsory reading was the New Zealand Herald's Wednesday travel section, where we picked up many helpful hints.

Our main aims were to meet people and to see how others lived, to start in Greece in the spring then move north towards England before the weather became too hot and uncomfortable and before the tourist spots became too crowded.

During the planning stage we walked a couple of miles each night before

We took with us around $2500 in United States dollars and sterling — plus some American and British currency which often came in handy, particularly on the last day in a country, when we didn't wish to change any more money.

We also had three different credit cards between us. These were very handy, as we purchased cash or more travellers' cheques with them.

Our daughter at home controlled these accounts and paid them from our funds which we had left invested, as they came due. This saved us from carrying large amounts of cash.

The Greek islands were the highlight of our trip and we visited 10 of them in the first eight weeks of our travels. They were very relaxing, each with its own charm and character. Our favourites were Santorini and Kalymnos (where we spent the Greek Easter) and the old

ranged from $8 to $20 a night.

Dining was usually the highpoint of our evenings. The numerous outdoor cafes offered a great variety of both Greek and European cuisine, and most islands produced their own wines, which were generally quite palatable, only one being in the "rough red" category. Dinner varied in price from $7 to $25, depending on appetite and surroundings.

Transport on the islands was either by bus, which was an adventure in itself and often produced comedy of a high calibre, or by hired pushbikes, or by walking. Our costs on the islands totalled $21 a day each.

We were apprehensive about our next stop, Turkey, but it was to provide us with a surprise. Turkey was the friendliest and, at $17 a day each, the cheapest country we visited. Later, Scandinavia was the dearest at around $50 a day, and in Oslo at an outdoor bar a pint of beer cost $9 (we shared one).

From Istanbul it took us 40 hours and four different buses to reach Dubrovnik in Yugoslavia. Arriving in the same clothes we left in and looking rather scruffy, we were glad to be met by a woman offering a room and shower.

We were pleased that our travel agent had advised getting a first-class Eurail ticket, as the

● View of the picturesque fishing village of Mevagissey in Cornwall, one of the many places visited on the tour.

second-class was usually very overcrowded. Once we got the hang of Eurail travel we found it excellent and didn't need to book.

On long journeys we always managed to obtain a compartment to ourselves and were able to stretch out in our sleeping bags.

Eurail took us from Vienna to Salzburg, Munich, Zurich, Lucerne, Liechtenstein, St Gallen, Luxembourg, Brussels, then on to Scandinavia and then back to Ostend to catch the hydrofoil to Dover.

Discount

In Britain we travelled by bus. At Victoria Station we obtained a one-month pass for $20 which gave a 33 percent discount on all National Express buses. We saved this amount on our first two trips, London-Huddersfield-Edinburgh.

This pass is available by showing a current New Zealand passport and is available for National Ex-

press bus travel in England, Scotland and Wales. We obtained two of these passes during our three months of travelling around the United Kingdom.

These travels took us from Dover to Inverness, by ship to the Isle of Man, and to Ireland — where we loved the countryside and the people. We visited Belfast, Donegal, Galway, Killarney, where we hitch-hiked to Cork, then to Dublin.

By ship to Holyhead, then through Wales to Bath, Devon, Cornwall (to the lovely fishing village of Mevagissey), back to London, Oxford, Stratford and then to Huddersfield, where we stayed for three months.

The cost for the three months of bus travel was only $1500 for both of us. Pub meals were well prepared and reasonably priced.

Through Europe and the United Kingdom we stayed in youth hostels (great for meeting people and obtaining informa-

tion), at bed-and-breakfast houses (good for sleeping late and for getting a little extra rest), private rooms and, in some places, with friends, including a pensfriend I had not written to for over 20 years.

Restful

We also spent nine days based in a relative's caravan in Ramsgate, which provided us with a much-needed rest when we first arrived in England.

We both had an internal frame backpack that converts into a suitcase and carries around 12kg-15kg of gear, plus an airline type carrybag. We also used our sleeping bags quite a lot and were glad to have them. We had sleep sheets too that are compulsory in most youth hostels.

Like most Kiwis who travel we usually wore tracksuit pants and road shoes with suitable sweat-tops. (You can spot a Kiwi anywhere when travel-

ling, by their tracksuit pants.)

Our 10-day trip home was from Gatwick to San Francisco, then on to Honolulu and Auckland.

Places we visited and events we attended included opera in Vienna, the Munich Zoo, Funen Village in Denmark, the Greek Easter celebrations, gymnasts in Sweden, the Commonwealth Games, soccer in Scotland and England, rugby in Wales, Gaelic football in Ireland, the Australian v Great Britain rugby league series.

What we had spent in 10½ months most people would spend on an eight to 18-week package tour. We struck no major hassles while travelling and found that with a little patience we usually reached our required destination and always finished up with a roof over our heads.

We often came across youngsters who thought it was great that people of their parents' age were travelling as we do.

NZ Herald, 5/8/87, 1200 Words

or overseas, the first thing people do is look around, a dead giveaway. Sometimes it is very handy to let locals know you come from New Zealand.

One afternoon on Santorini, Lynne and I were walking high in the hills on a path through an area that had been hit years before by an earthquake. A man was standing at his front gate. I'm fair headed, and he said, 'Deutsch,' taking me to be German, which happened several times in Europe. I replied, 'No, New Zealand.' With delight he said, 'Ah, Kiwi, you are all our friends, come in and have a drink.' We went into his house for a very enjoyable hour. Lynne loved the opportunity to see inside his home.

TRAVEL

If, as the saying goes, life begins at 40, there is still plenty of time to visit some interesting places without a detailed itinerary, as NORM STEPHENS discovered during travels with his wife, Lynne.

There can be the other side. On three occasions in the then, Yugoslavia I had women be very rude to me. I guessed they thought I was German. We have met many very friendly people I could write several chapters about.

It is said, the best thing about travel is the planning, then on return, telling everyone about your wonderful experiences.

Sadly, COVID has savaged the world tourist trade. We are both pleased we have seen what we have. I'm glad we are here, home in our own beautiful New Zealand.

Part 2

Part two is a series of fictional short stories, mostly written during the 1990s.

Norm (60), favourite seat at bach before renovations, kitchen behind and fantastic view to the front - 1996

The Great Village Chariot Race

To celebrate the end of level four and complete lockdown due to the COVID-19 pandemic, a race was announced by Libby and for all residents of the Waiheke Retirement Village who had a mobility scooter to compete on.

Libby called a meeting of the residents who owned these vehicles. She told us she was the organiser and sole judge, and her decision would be final, with no appeals allowed (she who must be obeyed). Libby had allocated all relevant personnel. Gary was the starter and track marshall. Lindsay, because he was a JP, was judge of results as no photo finish camera was available.

Janet and Jan were lap counters. Dane was to marshal the workshop turn around and Jack and Ray were to marshal the two corners at each end of the duck pond. The course was to start at the village entrance with a long straight to the turnaround (an empty drum) opposite the swimming pool where the officials would sit. The distance was twenty laps.

The start would be Grand Prix style with two carts wide, staggered by four carts long, the last car at the edge of the road. The drivers were all issued with a number that represented their carts and start positions. Libby maintained they had been drawn out of a hat, but I had my doubts. I decided not to protest even though I drew number eight, the black marker.

After the meeting, I went home to study the field. Number one was Brenda; number two was Bob. I knew they were very experienced at this type of racing due to their winning a number of races on their Cruises. They were known to tandem race –one getting in front and the other slowing the rest down, then sharing the prize. Number three was Kara, also very experienced and known for her 'lead foot.' She had competed in the famous Greenham Common event, as well known as the Isle of Man Race. Also, the Cross America Long Distance Race where she finished a creditable third.

Jill who had recently borrowed the RSA scooter, was allocated Number four. She was the least experienced driver and would be making her debut. Number five was Ian who had won several events on a number of different tracks, was known to go hard and was favourite. I decided I would work my way to get behind him. Number six was Anne and number seven was Betty, both inexperienced and I was number eight. Although I had played many sports, I hadn't been in a chariot race like this. The winning prize was a silver cup, a bottle of champagne, and a big chocolate marshmallow Easter egg.

The day was sunny. The tide in Anzac Bay was tranquil. The carts proceeded to the start after a parade down the straight before a massive record crowd of fifty other residents. Brenda and Bob were both confident in their latest blue machines, dressed in blue overalls and flying blue pennants won on their previous races. Kara's machine was green, and she wore a rainbow stripped jacket and green pennant. Jill wore her husband's old Waitemata rugby jersey. Ian's machine was red, and adorned with his boat club pennant. Anne and Betty were both quite nervous about it all and were more demure in their everyday outfits. I wore a Warriors footie jersey and Warrior pennant.

Gary sent off the 3pm start. The thunder of the machines echoed around the valley as all eight kept their fingers on their warning bells as they went up the first long run to cheers from the crowd. The race started as I predicted with Brenda leading and Bob behind keeping to the middle of the road to make it hard to pass. Kara kept close, picking up valuable ground on the short straight, Jill close behind.

Ian was maneuvering around gradually getting in behind Bob. I followed him as close as I could as I knew I had to have patience. Betty and Anne, not being used to the hell for leather racing of the others, slowly dropped back and pulled out after twelve laps

Over the next five laps there were several changes as Ian took the lead and looked like being the eventual winner with Brenda and Kara close behind him. Bob's machine started playing up and he had to pull out. Jill was having a few problems and slipped back. I was starting to feel confident as I bided my time. Then, unbelievably, Ian a clear leader, failed to do the U-turn outside the workshop and went straight up the path towards his unit. I was amazed, maybe he had a memory blank, and thought the day was over.

Never look a gift horse in the mouth, I thought, time to take advantage and I had five laps to achieve it. I had noticed Kara slowed slightly as she went over the grating on the small rise to the workshop. I got close, then went hard on her inside as we hit the rise. I headed straight for the workshop marker, which forced her wide.

The last target was Brenda, two laps to go. I managed to get her inside and she went a little too wide as we came in the straight. Great, I had the lead with one lap to go. I kept the pressure on as we left the straight, slowing down on the last bends knowing she couldn't get around me and not leaving space to come inside me.

As we turned the last corner and headed down the short street, I knew I had it won. I could see the cup sitting on my bookshelf in front of the photo of the winner. I could taste the champagne (although I would rather have a beer). I could taste that lovely Easter egg.

Then bugger, I was roused from my daydreams by the sound of the kettle boiling it was 2020, a pandemic, and we were housebound.

Snow's Thunder House

Snow's 'Hillside Home' hadn't changed in the two years Artie and Sally had spent backpacking around Europe. Only Snow's close friends knew which large puriri tree marked where the track led to his pine planked hut. Unless one unexpectedly stumbled on his abode, while wandering through the bush, or zoned in on the continuous wisp of wood smoke that wafted from his chimney, it was nearly impossible to find Snow's home.

Artie had got to know Snow nearly thirty years before, when his best mate, Snow's son, the only child of a very short marriage, took him to visit when they were both seventeen. John had only seen his father on a few rare occasions since his mother had left Snow.

Fortunately, John could still remember where the path was when they went in search of his father. It had been a day that Artie would never forget, a balmy late summer Sunday. The two boys had sat out on the terrace looking at the view, and having their first taste of homebrew beer while listening to the wood pigeons and tuis in the nearby bush. It was also Artie's first experience of the 'Thunder House,' Snow's long drop toilet that was situated at the bottom of his vegetable garden.

The structure was built of rough sawn timber. The corrugated iron roof had seen better days but it managed to keep the rain out. Plastic strips hung in the doorway, swaying gently in the breeze.

A smooth wooden board with the appropriate hole was the seat, with more bugs visible inside the Thunder House than outside. The plastic strips were affectionately called by Snow, his elephant door.

'Would keep a herd of elephant out, that door would. Where else can you get a view like that when one's going about his business? Why spoil it putting a door there. No one can see in anyway.' Snow had proudly told them.

High on the hill overlooking Onetangi Bay, the property had a magnificent view of the beach and the western end of the island. Rangitoto and the city were away to the south, to the north was a panoramic view of Great Barrier, Little Barrier and Kawau Islands.

People didn't visit Snow. They were either taken there by Snow, or were a close friend who knew he would be welcome. When guys were getting on his wick in the local boozer, Snow would invite them to try his 'Hillside Brew' on the following Sunday. Usually, they set off up the steep hill and searched in vain. Snow had told them, 'Can't miss it, about a mile up the road on the left, just past the fifth lamp post, there's a sign on the tree, 'Snow's Hillside Home' just follow the track, can't miss it.' Snow never mentioned that the sign had disappeared over twenty years before.

The cunning old codger probably took it down himself. If they ever managed to finally stumble onto his home, Snow reckoned they must be a good sort. He would greet them with a cheeky grin and a handle of homebrew.

Snow's hut consisted of one big room, which contained two bunks, a table and two chairs, a few cupboards and a sink. A bookshelf completly covered one wall. Dominating one end, a wood range, his pride and joy, provided his heat, hot water and cooking. When electricity came to the island, Snow refused to have the power connected. To this day the place remained as it was. John reckoned this was why his mother left. She was sick of living in such a small place without the commodity considered a necessity in most households.

John had left for Australia a few years after that first visit. Snow always made Artie welcome and he had enjoyed many hours in

Snow's company listening to his stories about Waiheke. The two had regularly gone on long hikes over the island. Artie was always amazed that Snow could find so many interesting places and people to call on.

For his part Snow treated the younger man as a brother, even though there was a twenty-year age difference. He looked forward to Artie's visits, listening intently to his travel stories, and postcards Artie had sent were pinned over his bunk.

'Don't get many from John, usually around Christmas and my birthday, which is better than nothing I suppose,' Snow had once remarked.

Snow and Artie shared the same birth sign. This visit was a special one. Snow was to be seventy the following week, Artie, fifty. Two days later, Artie made the hike up the hill on the Sunday morning eager to see his old friend. He had a gift of a book by one of Snow's favourite authors. Over the years Artie had added many books to Snow's collection. Artie had told his wife, Sally, to expect him later in the afternoon, warning her he would probably be a little the worse for wear.

As Artie approached the hut, he gave his usual whistle. He was delighted to hear Snow answer.

'Was wondering what time you'd be here, just opened one, thought you'd be thirsty, come in, we'll go out on the terrace and you can tell me all about your trip, that is, what you didn't put in all those postcards you sent, must've cost a fortune.' Snow paused. 'How the hell are you anyway?'

By this time Artie had shaken hands and was seated on the terrace with his own special handle in his hand, a present Snow had given him on his twenty-first birthday. The handle was not allowed to leave the hut and no one else was allowed to use it.

Snow's thick head of silver hair gave him a distinguished appearance. The scar from his days as a boxer was still visible over his left eye. He stood very straight, looking as fit as when Artie had first met him over thirty years before. He still retained that impish grin that had become a trademark, the blue eyes, still clear.

Several stories and brews later, Artie excused himself to visit the Thunder House. It was in the same place, a slight lean to one side of the timber-planked structure was the only significant change Artie noticed.

'See your door is still keeping the elephants out, and the view is still the best.' Artie said on his return.

'Been a great servant that in me hour of need. Strike anything like that in your travels?' Snow asked.

'There's only one Thunder House in the world like that, Snow. They threw away the mould when you built it.' Artie could see the proud grin splash across the older man's face at this complimentary remark. 'Mind you, Snow, we tried out some pretty unusual small rooms in our walkabouts.'

'Tell me about them.' Snow asked enthusiastically. 'But wait a minute, I'll take a couple of caps off me latest special brew. I still keep the bad brews for those bludgers who I invite and hope they don't come but get here despite my directions.' Snow filled their empty handles. 'Did you come across any of those bidet things?'

'Yes, Snow, most hotels in European countries have them. Sally had an experience with one, made me laugh, but caused her some embarrassment. She was looking at the bidet with much trepidation, then pushed the button while peering down the bowl. The water shot up and hit her in the eye and wet her hair. I beat her to the bar by twenty minutes as she had to dry her hair.'

'Bet she wasn't too happy with you laughing at her.'

'No sense of humour these women, Snow. Mind you, those bidets were handy for rinsing out our undies and socks. After all it was fresh water.' Before Snow had a chance to comment, Artie continued. 'Biggest fright I got was one night in a pension in Turkey. I was in the universal position thinking about the world, when there was an almighty bang. I thought their arch enemies, the Greeks, had attacked.' Artie stopped for a sip.

'Go on mate, what happened?'

'When Sally turned on the hot tap over the hand basin, it activated the flame that fired the gas califont into action. It was situated right beside where I was sitting much to my discomfort. Stupid place to have the gas anyway.'

'I bet Sally laughed at you, got her revenge there, mate.' Snow added.

'Yeah, she got one back on me, Snow.' Artie was warmed up to his subject and carried on. 'Biggest bathroom we came across was in a three-hundred-year-old pub in Leeds. There was a plaque in the bar downstairs to say Dick Turpin, the highwayman, had often stayed there. The bathroom and toilet were bigger than your home, the old bath was that large I reckon Dick Turpin's horse could've drowned in it. On the other end of the scale was the bed and breakfast place we stayed at in a Cornish fishing village. The toilet was built into an old cupboard. I had to back in, and I'm not that big. I doubt if any of our All Black forwards could even get in, let alone sit down.'

'My old Thunder House sounds pretty good to me,' Snow said after a short break to the topic of conversation.

'Your Thunder House is a palace compared to some we had the misfortune to encounter,' Artie replied.

Artie had stayed longer than usual. The sun would soon be disappearing over the hills at the other end of the bay and he decided it was time to take his leave. This was no simple task. By the time he had one for the road, then one for the gutter, finally one for nothing at all, darkness was descending rapidly. He knew Sally would be wondering if they were getting up to their old tricks by making a night of it.

'I better spend a penny and give my regards to the Thunder House before I hit the track.' Artie said as he tripped over an empty crate on the way out the door.

Snow was standing on the terrace when Artie returned. 'Won't come up the track with you, mate, you know your way out, guess I can trust you not to get lost in the bush.' Snow offered his hand and shook Artie's strongly. 'Guess I'll be seeing more of you this coming summer seeing you and Sally won't be traipsing around the world. I'll make a special brew for your next visit.'

Artie thanked his friend for his hospitality and walked up the path to the darkened road feeling that he had detected a small tear in Snow's eye as they exchanged farewells. Must be the beer Artie thought, feeling light-headed, or feeling no pain, as Snow usually exclaimed when they had had, one, or two, over the eight. The two miles back to his own home seemed to take no time at all.

Sally gave Artie a hard knowing look. She was like that. One stare from his wife was worth a thousand words.

'Snow sends his regards. He's looking pretty fit. The old Thunder House still has the magnificent view.' Artie realized he was prattling on. Fortunately dinner was soon on the table. Conversation turned to more mundane happenings than Artie's pilgrimage to his old mate's Hillside Home.

Several Sundays later Artie received a call from Snow's neighbour Jimmy. 'Sorry to tell you, I have some bad news for you. Snow's dead.' Jimmy hesitated, realizing Artie had received a shock, then carried on. 'Snow didn't turn up to the boozer yesterday. Tom and I went up there this morning and found him. Can you get hold of his son in Australia?'

Artie said he would ring immediately.

It was with much trepidation that Artie walked down the track to the familiar old hut. With him was the local policeman, Jimmy and Tom. When they entered the hut the policeman took over the proceedings. He announced that the doctor had found Snow died of natural causes. As Artie had been a long-time friend and regular visitor would he have a look around, in case there was anything missing, or untoward. He was fairly satisfied everything was in order, although he wanted to be assured so he could finalise his report.

Artie was glad that they had taken Snow away. He preferred to remember him as he last saw him. It took only a few moments to see everything was as Snow kept it.

It was not until he walked outside and looked down towards the bay, he realized the Thunder House was gone.

At first it was with disbelief to discover it had completely disappeared. Only the bare earth remained where the structure had stood, the long drop hole had been filled with fresh earth and a small native tree planted there. Artie looked around. There was no trace of the timber boards, or roofing iron that had withstood the ravages of the weather over the years.

'What do you make of that?' the policeman asked.

'I don't really know. Snow loved a joke and a bit of a mystery. Maybe this was his way of saying good-bye.' Artie replied. The four men returned inside the hut. Artie noticed the crate of Snow's Special Brew. Around the neck of each bottle was a small piece of small plastic from the elephant door.

After the funeral John and Artie returned to the hut, sat out on the Terrace and opened one of Snow's Special Brews, Artie stood and raised his handle. 'I propose a toast. To Snow, the Thunder House, pleasant memories and the great times I had here.' The two men clinked handles and drank to Snow.

They sat silently for some time, quietly drinking, each thinking his own thoughts. One of the man who was his father, the other of the man who was more like a brother.

Artie broke the silence, 'You know, John, I can almost feel Snow's presence here with us. It's as if he's having a laugh at our expense. I remember the last time I saw him, when we parted he had a small tear in his eye, and he shook my hand very strongly.

That night the two friends walked away from the Hillside Home feeling no pain.

Flounder Flats

Artie knew as soon as he walked in the Onetangi Pub on the Saturday afternoon it was going to be one of those weekends. His mate, Snow was propped against the bar in his favourite spot, pint in hand with a big grin over his face.

'See you're on your own, mate. I'll get you a beer.'

'With that smile I'd say you've got a walkabout planned.'

Snow handed Artie his beer. 'You gave me the inspiration when you walked in.' Artie was well aware that Snow loved to give the impression that their walkabouts were spontaneous ideas. Deep down he always had a feeling that Snow had pre-planned the idea and was hoping Artie would turn up at the pub on his own.

'What've you got in mind, Snow?'

'Well, mate,' Artie had always been mate to Snow ever since they had met on the day the pub opened thirty years before. Artie had been single then; Snow had remained a bachelor. The two had become great friends and their pranks and walkabouts had become pub legends.

Snow continued. 'I don't think you've met Old George, World War Two veteran who lives on his own down at Flounder Flats.'

Here we go again, Artie thought. Flounder Flats, I've never heard that place mentioned before, obviously another of Snow's made-up names.

'Never heard of Flounder Flats, Snow, where's that?'

'Past the mountain and down the Scotsman's fence line to the backwater. You've been down the Scotsman's Farm, mate. It's in that direction.'

This was another of Snow's habits, using his own place names. Some were common to Artie. He knew where the Scotsman's Farm was. Even though the Scotsman had been gone a dozen years, it was still the Scotsman's Farm to Snow.

Snow was well revved up and full of enthusiasm. 'Tell you what mate, stay at my place tonight and we'll get an early start in the morning. Don't worry about dinner, I've got plenty of food and the fridge is full of homebrew. Right, that's settled, let's get down to some serious drinking. I think it's your shout.'

Artie got their beers and they settled in for the afternoon.

Next morning Artie awoke to the smell of bacon and eggs. Snow was bustling around the kitchen, glass of homebrew in one hand, egg splice in the other.

'Come on, mate, time to get moving do you want a reviver? You certainly packed a few away last night.'

The thought of a beer that early in the morning was the last thing on Artie's mind. 'No thanks, Snow, bacon and eggs and a coffee will be fine. I'll be up in a minute.' Artie knew it would be a long, hard day. He had never been able to match Snow's habit to have a beer first thing in the morning after a heavy night.

Snow soon had breakfast on the table. 'Get that down you. It'll take over two hours to get to the flats, 'specially as we've got a fair load to carry.'

Between the two of them they packed beer cans, batteries, canned food, steak, sausages, books, magazines, and other items Snow kept shoving in.

'I've left some beers on the top, we'll need a few pit stops on the way. It's going to be a hot one,' Snow said.

'Better tell me a bit about this George guy, Snow,' said Artie.

'I'll tell you about him as we hit the trail.'

George had signed for the army soon after war broke out. He had seen action in Greece, Crete, North Africa and was in Italy when hostilities ended. When he came home, he drifted from job to job. Then he fell madly in love, which settled him down for a good year. When he thought everything was roses, his girlfriend became pregnant. Her family had never liked George as he was ten years older and had a reputation as a local tearaway. They moved her away and had the child adopted out. George was devastated as they had both been keen to marry. He never saw her again.

The next summer he crewed on a yacht around Waiheke. One weekend they were down the flats and George told his mates that was the place for him. The next week they dropped him off with a small tent and some gear. When they went back six weeks later, he informed them he was staying for good. George had come to an agreement that he would look after the stock and fences at the flats and keep the boaties and their dogs away in return for a few provisions.

Later the Scotsman carted down an army hut that were popular around the island at that time. George has lived in it to this day. The Scotsman had gone but subsequent farmers had carried on the agreement.

They reached George's old hut, surrounded by a large vegetable garden and orchard, by late morning. Old sheets of corrugated iron formed a square around the area.

'Keeps the sheep and the rabbits out,' Snow offered.

There didn't appear to be anyone around. 'Jeez he's dead.' Artie blurted out as he followed Snow through the open door to see a thin, suntanned naked body on the bed.

'Who's the family ghost, Snow?' The body said, as it stood up wrapping a towel around his middle, greeting Snow with a handshake.

'This is an old mate of mine. George, meet Artie.'

Artie was still getting over the shock of seeing George stretched out. He had genuinely thought he was dead.

'Just having a snooze, been out in the garden since sun-up, had a feeling you might make it today, seeing tomorrow's a holiday. Come on let's go outside and enjoy the sunshine.'

The three went out on to the veranda, sitting down on a variety of makeshift seats. Snow handed out the beer, and then took the contents out of the two packs.

'Every day's Christmas when Snow comes here.' George enthused. 'I'll light up the fire later and we'll have a slap-up lunch. You can add a flounder to that steak and sausages you brought, plus I've got a couple of my Mountain Dew in the fridge to wash it down.'

'Where's the fridge?' Artie asked, having noticed there was only a battery-operated radio inside the hut.

'Come, I'll show you,' George said getting up.

'I'll go and get a few rock oranges for entrée.' Snow said as he moved away. 'Caught my first flounder here, mate.'

Artie guessed that's how Snow gave it the name Flounder Flats. George took Artie up a hill behind the hut where a waterfall, fed from a spring, fell into a large pool. George reached down into the water. Artie watched him open a metal box-type affair and pull out a bottle.

'Not a bad fridge eh! This pool is my drinking water. We've piped it down to the hut. That pool down there is my bath, go in every day. I don't want for anything here. All the fruit and vegetables I need, plenty of fish and flounder, even get a feed of mussels and oysters, or rock oranges as Snow calls them. Farmer drops me in a bit of mutton, I live like a king. Come on let's go and light the fire, Snow'll be back soon.'

The hours raced as they ate heartily, washed down with beer and George's pumpkin wine. George told Artie about the war and his early days in Point Chevalier. Snow had heard it all before. George asked Artie about his life. He was interested to know he was adopted. Artie had been born in Christchurch and moved to Auckland at an early age. A few days before he was married, his parents told him he was adopted. At twenty-six he felt it was too late to seek his birth parents.

'You know Artie you are the same age as my son, but he was born in Wellington three months before you. I sometimes wonder what he is like,' George said.

Snow stood up. 'Come on, mate, the sun's going down. It'll be dark when we get back. See you George, look after yourself.'

'Thanks for coming, Snow. Bring Artie back again.' The old war veteran shook their hands, turned away into his hut. They had walked a short distance when George called Snow back to the hut.

Artie chattered to Snow all the way back about the old man.

It was a year before Artie met George again. On several occasions he had tried to get Snow to go down to the flats. But Snow always had an excuse. 'Went a couple of weeks ago, you know George, too many visits and I'll outstay my welcome.'

Artie had thought about going down on his. However, on the way back Snow had returned by a different route. Snow was always going to places one way and returning another. Artie was never sure Snow did it to show his knowledge of the island, or to make the destination a mystery.

'George was asking after you the last time I was down, mate.' Snow remarked as they set out on their hike to the flats.

'Somehow I think his seventy plus years are staring to catch up on him.'

Artie could see the difference as George greeted them. He was sitting on his favourite seat on the veranda. He waited until they had reached the hut before standing. George was thinner than before and he wore a thick bush shirt even though the day was warm. The garden was overgrown and the inside of the hut untidy.

George bucked up noticeably as they hauled their bounty out of the packs. After Snow cooked a meal, George picked at his food and drank sparsely.

'I don't know,' George said agitatedly. 'Every news bulletin I hear the Government seems to be either giving the land back to the Maoris or selling our assets to foreigners. I thought we went to war to save our country, now these bludgers are giving it away. I must be getting old.'

Snow and Artie took their leave early. It was obvious that George was tiring. Their walk back was a quiet one, each thinking their own thoughts about the old recluse.

Four weeks later Artie received a call from Snow. George had died. Could he come to Waiheke the next weekend to scatter his ashes at the flats. Artie agreed.

The walk out passed quickly. Snow explained that the farmer had demolished the old hut as he was worried vandals may set fire to it. After they had scattered the ashes, Snow produced a bottle of George's wine.

'The last one, mate. Let's drink to George.'

As they sat quietly drinking, Snow handed a small tin to Artie.

'George wanted you to have this.'

Artie cautiously opened the tin. On top was George's war medals, then his birth certificate and army pay book, several photos of George in army uniform, a photo of George and a woman, and lastly one of the woman on her own.

Artie froze. He had never seen her before, yet her features appeared familiar. He studied the photo for several minutes before reading the solicitor's letter that explained he was George's son. The enclosed cheque was for half of his estate, the other half went to Snow. Artie looked at the cheque. It was for a lot of money. He looked straight at Snow.

'I think you've got some explaining to do my old mate.'

Snow had been closely watching Artie. He was ready.

'George recognized you the minute you walked in to the hut. As you can see, you're the spitting image of your mother. When you told him you were adopted and gave your date and place of birth, he knew.'

'But George said there was three months difference.'

'George was pretty quick there; he gave you his date of birth and made up the Wellington bit. Remember how he called me back. That's when he swore me to secrecy. I contacted his solicitor, brother Ted, who is the only one who has had anything to do with George, the rest disowned him.'

'Ted had always admired George for his war service. He looked up to him as a hero and handled George's money. I became their go-between. George never touched a cracker of his pension. He always said he would give me half his fortune when he died, I always thought it was his little joke. I think we'd better head back and have a quiet celebration.'

Neither uttered a single word on the walk back. It wasn't until they were seated in Snow's house that Artie realized they had returned by the same route.

Note on the Text

This story won the 1994 Waiheke Writers Group short story competition. The presentation was held at what is now the Oyster Inn. I was dressed more for a sports function, in summer longs, complete opposite to most of the gathering. Some men looked like Earnest Hemmingway, long scruffy hair, full beard, turtle neck pullover, jeans or cords and sandals. A couple even wore berets.

The story, though fiction, is based on fact. Eddie had been told the story of a man who lived at the head of Te Matuku Bay estuary. What decade and for what reason he was there we had no idea. In the 1960s we found where his hut had been. All that was left was the concrete steps and a few wooden posts that marked the section. There were the remnants of three fruit trees in an area that looked like it had been an orchard. One didn't need much imagination to see how he would have lived.

A woman at the event accosted me and said, 'I know just the man you wrote about. I've seen him. I had a bit of a quiet laugh. She was only in her late thirties. She wouldn't have been alive when we had found the site, which I guessed had been vacated for at least twenty years before that.

Their Beach

*J*immy gazed around the interior of the caravan. He and Sarah had always dreamed of camping by a beach, waking to the pounding of the waves, surf casting, catching fish, fossicking amongst the flotsam thrown up by the tide, and long walks along their beach in the evenings.

'Everything here a man needs,' he thought. 'Everything, except the caravan parked in my son's backyard.' Jimmy shrugged. He sat brooding, his mind going over the past four years. 'All that planning for nought, no beach, just a caravan in a backyard in the middle of suburbia.'

Three years before, when Sarah died, his son and daughter-in-law suggested he come to live with them. He had agreed on the condition he would be self-sufficient and look after himself.

'You two don't want me under your feet all day, you have your own lives to live. This way we can each have our privacy yet be near enough when needed.' Jimmy had stated.

The arrangement had worked well. He had kept his independence and the grandchildren gave him much pleasure, plus a little heartache. Justin, now six, had been very close to Sarah. Often, he would say, 'I miss my nana, she was my bestest friend ever.'

'Yes, Justin, she was my best friend too,' Jimmy would reply.

Kylie was one, when Sarah died, she would sometimes ask,

'Where did my nana go to, Grandad?'

Justin usually answered, 'To Heaven of course.'

It was at these times Jimmy would think of his wife, but the thoughts would go back further than that fateful day when Sarah suffered heart failure, brought on by an asthma attack. Married in their late twenties, their early years had been a struggle as both had spent their savings on travel. Both New Zealand born, they had met in London, toured Europe together then returned home to marry. Jimmy secured a position as head store man in a local carpet manufacturing plant. They raised two children and finally paid off their own home.

The two brothers who owned the carpet company, the accountant, their solicitor, and a few longer-term employees had set up a share club. On the advice of their solicitor only days before the share market crash, they had fortunately sold a large parcel of their shares for a good price. At this stage they all agreed to wind up the club and sell their remaining share for the best price they could obtain. Over the years the club had operated, they had made a healthy profit, usually through the solicitor's direction.

A year later, the two brothers then approaching their seventies, sold the company to a major corporation. At that stage Jimmy and Sarah decided to purchase a townhouse, then they would get their dream caravan and look for the right beach for their future retirement.

Tom, the company solicitor, had become their legal representative and close friend. He agreed with their decision. Their house sold quickly, and they moved into a small, rented unit, they paid a deposit on a townhouse under construction. The balance of their money they left with Tom to hold in a trust fund.

Jimmy and Sarah were enjoying life. Most weekends they would head off in the car looking for a beach then staying overnight in a local motel. They had seen the caravan they wanted but held off on the purchase until the townhouse was completed.

The first major blow came one Friday afternoon. The carpet factory staffs were called to the lunchroom. The new manager was sorry to announce that the factory would be closing immediately. All machinery was to be moved out of the Auckland area and the entire staff would be laid off. They would each be given an envelope with their final pay, plus a small redundancy payment that was not negotiable and a reference. They were told to clear their lockers and leave the premises within thirty minutes. The staff were stunned. They completed their final formalities like zombies.

'Bloody sorry all right,' Jimmy announced as they left the factory. 'They had worked everything to the last detail, asset stripping, we didn't stand a chance. Thirty years of work, all over in thirty minutes. Not even a decent send off.'

Jimmy went home and discussed the situation with Sarah. They felt they could cope. The townhouse was covered by the money held in trust by Tom, plus a bit over. Jimmy had put the money from the share club into bonus bonds to cover the cost of the caravan. Sarah had a part-time job; Jimmy was confident he would get a job to cover the next three years until he retired.

Two months later another bombshell struck. Jimmy was jobless and the prospects of employment dim. The townhouse was nearing completion when a letter arrived from the development company stating that payment was overdue. Jimmy was not worried by the letter, a small oversight on Tom's part, was his immediate reaction. But after two days ringing Tom's office and being put off by his secretary, he became concerned.

It was late afternoon when Jimmy arrived at Tom's office. He was not alone. Several very agitated people were waiting. The secretary kept repeating she was sorry she didn't know where Mr. O'Brien was, but a representative was coming soon.

'I'll bet he's shot through.' Someone angrily shouted.

The noise was reaching a crescendo when a dark suited man and a uniformed security officer arrived. The security man called for silence. 'Mr. Jamieson from the bank will make a statement.'

'I'm sorry to announce that Mr. O'Brien has been put into receivership by the bank. We can't divulge the amount outstanding. At this moment we have alerted the police to his disappearance.

Now if you could please leave as there is nothing more we can do at this time.'

The gathered crowd were angry, the secretary was crying, and the security man was trying to get people to leave. Two newspaper reporters and a photographer arrived. Jimmy could see it all. 'The bastard's gone and probably our townhouse too.' He walked out in a daze.

Sarah was shattered. Jimmy had never wanted to leave the money with Tom, but Sarah had insisted. 'Better interest rates than the bank and he is our friend.'

Over the following year Sarah developed asthma and Tom was arrested in Australia by the fraud squad. Their townhouse was gone, and Jimmy was still jobless. Then Sarah suddenly died.

When Jimmy first took up residence in the caravan he kept dwelling on the past year, losing his job, then their savings, then Sarah. He and Sarah had done everything together.

The guys he knew at his local club were never that close, in fact most of them were a pain. It was a blow up at the club that finally got him out of his depression. The usual half dozen guys were sitting around the same table telling the same stories. Jimmy had heard them a thousand times, and he casually remarked. 'That new publican at the Central had done a good job. I've called there a few times lately, quite a friendly place now.'

'Who wants to drink with those dole bludgers!' Leo blurted.

'Bunch of layabouts, work if you want it,' stated Johnny.

'Wouldn't know what a hard day's work was.' added Alan.

Jimmy had had enough. He took a deep breath, looked hard at his companions around the table then exploded. 'You guys are always on about the young ones on the dole. If some of you were just leaving school, you wouldn't get a job either. I seem to remember, Leo, that you were always on compo, or on strike, and you Alan was always skiting about ripping your bosses off. You forget that I'm on the dole. I've tried to get work, but they don't want you when you're coming up to sixty. You lot want to be thankful you're on the pension.'

The Duty officer came over to the table. Jimmy saw him coming and stood up. 'No need to get excited, Fred. I'm leaving, and I won't be back. This place is like an old folk's home, everyone in the same place telling the same boring stories. I'm off to where there's a bit of life.'

Clare frowned, 'We've been a bit worried about you lately.'

Jimmy laughed, 'Don't worry, I should've told that lot to stick it a long time ago. I've now come to grips with losing Sarah and our savings. Things never turn out as you plan. I'll be on the pension soon. I've got the caravan and a few savings. We all get on okay. I've got the garden and the grandkids. The sun's shining. What more do I need?'

The next two years went well for Jimmy, he felt he had a new purpose in life. On one of his forays to the local park with Justin and Kylie he met a young Polynesian guy. The lad was having difficulties at home. He had no job and had been before the court on several minor police charges. Jimmy and young Jimmy Joe became good friends.

One day Jimmy Joe confessed to the older man, 'You're the only one I can talk to Jimmy. Dad's always on the booze. Mum's at Housie and my older brothers and sisters have left home. My mates are only interested in stealing and smoking dope.'

Jimmy spent hours in the park talking to Jimmy Joe. He could pick his mood changes, sometimes positive, mostly despondent. He also knew that when he became aggressive he had been out with his mates. The older man tried to get Jimmy Joe away from them, but deep down he knew that his friend was under the influence of the leader, Jake.

Jimmy went to the Central Hotel on a Wednesday afternoon. He was made welcome by the publican and enjoyed the company of the patrons. He had a few small bets on the TAB, usually taking his and Sarah's favourite numbers in quinellas. On the way home he would buy takeaways for his dinner.

One day when he was on his way to the Central, Jimmy Joe called out. 'Hey, Jimmy, I've got some good news, I'm starting a course at

Polytech on Monday.'

'That's great,' enthused the older man. 'Now that you've got a chance to make the most of it, try and keep away from Jake.'

Jimmy had a good day at the hotel winning over two hundred dollars on the races. He shouted drinks and left later than usual. At the takeaway bar, he noticed Jimmy Joe waiting down the road. He waved and moved towards him.

'Hi Jimmy Joe. I'm a bit late tonight. I've had a good day.'

Jimmy noticed the young Polynesian was crying, and then he heard Jake's demanding voice.

'Go on, Jimmy Joe. Tell the old man we want his money.'

Jimmy could tell his friend was under Jake's power. Jimmy turned to remonstrate with Jake but was pushed to the ground by another teenager standing next to the leader. Jake's eyes were glazed, he looked mean, in his big hands was a baseball bat.

'Get the money, Jimmy Joe. Don't be chicken,' Jake shouted.

Jimmy Joe blubbered. 'Don't hurt him. He's my friend. He's an old man.'

Jimmy looked at Jimmy Joe becoming more aggressive he had a sinking feeling in his stomach of disaster. The first kick in his back from Jake sent a tremendous pain through his entire body.

'Hurry up, old man. Give us your money,' Jake spat out.

Jimmy's back hurt, he could see Sarah where Jimmy Joe was standing. He was kicked again. He reached for Sarah's hand, but it was Jimmy Joe's fist. Jimmy tasted the blood in his mouth. Sarah was there again. The baseball bat crashed down on his head. He felt blood oozing down under his collar. His head hurt.

'Sorry, Sarah, that things didn't go to plan for us, but I had a good day today. Justin still misses his bestest friend and Kylie's a little princess. We'll all go for a walk when I get home.' Jimmy was burbling. Every bone in his body ached. He was drifting. His three tormentors were in a frenzy, screaming madly, wildly punching and kicking. Sirens wailed in the distance. Very vaguely he heard Jake's commanding voice.

'We better split - the cops are coming!'

The baseball bat smashed down on his head for the final time. Jimmy was completely oblivious to the three youths trying to run away from the police. He never heard the ambulance arrive. He was happily walking hand in hand with Sarah along their beach.

Last Swim

*S*id's shrieking woke Jack out of his deep alcoholic sleep. 'Blasted seagull, he won't shut up until I feed him.' Jack got out of bed slowly, his head was thick, his mouth dry. He opened the big double lounge window and leaned on the sill. The seagull was perched on the terrace balcony looking down his beak at Jack.

'Hey, come on, Sid, not you too. You don't have to look at me like that. I thought I got enough advice and knowing looks over the weekend from the old girl. Hold on and I'll get some bread, so don't give me a hard time.'

Jack returned, broke the bread into several pieces then laid it along the window sill and stood back a pace.

'There you are, Sid, better get stuck in before the sparrows come. Sorry I'm late, mate, but I had a tough Easter. Not every day your missus gives you the push. At least you haven't deserted me. I see Old Ma Johnson is checking up on us.' Jack realized he was rambling on.

Feeding Sid had become a morning ritual. Usually, Jack was up before seven and opening the large window. Within minutes Sid could be seen flying in circles towards the terrace where he would strut along the balcony while waiting for his bread. Any other seagull who dared to land on the terrace was soon dispatched by Sid, amid much noise and flapping of wings. On occasions like today when

Jack was late, Sid would start shrieking to get his attention.

The noise usually brought his neighbour by the reserve, Old Ma Johnson out on to her terrace. She reminded Jack of Sid as she looked up at his house, head forward, slightly tilted as she squinted to see what the fuss was about. She didn't miss much even though she reckoned she was losing her sight.

The seagull was going through his usual manoeuvres. It gulped down a large piece, then went into several aerobic convulsions to get the bread down into his gullet. The exercise was repeated until all the bread was gone at which point Sid took off, gracefully gliding over Ma Johnson's cottage towards the beach.

Jack made the bed, shaved, then prepared breakfast. He sat at the double window looking out to sea as he drank his coffee.

'At least I've still got this view and my name's not on the back page of todays newspaper. I may be broke, but I don't owe anyone any money. I thought my wife was going to give me a medal for long service, not the heave-ho.'

Anne, Jack's wife of thirty-five years, had come to the beach for the Easter holidays. Since Jack had been made redundant two years before, their marriage had gone through several upheavals, culminating in a mutual agreement to live apart. Anne in the city unit, Jack at the bach.

Jack had looked forward to Easter as he hadn't seen Anne for several weeks. However, it was not the reunion he had hoped for. They had disagreed over the most minor matters. Saturday had been a no-speak-day. Then Sunday, Anne surprised Jack when she stated quite unemotionally, without even a tear. 'I'm not coming back to the beach again. It's obvious you don't want to come back to town, you would rather be a beach bum. All you seem to care about it is your fishing, your garden, your homebrew and your mates at the pub. I'm sick of this beach. I've been coming here since I was born. I don't care if I never see it again.'

That was it, one small speech. Jack never disagreed. Somehow, he knew it was inevitable. They quietly discussed and surprisingly agreed on a few points. On Monday Anne caught the midday bus back to town.

After seeing Anne to the bus stop, Jack walked along the beach, deep in thought he never saw the bus go past. 'I should've stopped her. No, she had made up her mind. We'd both made up our minds. Let's face it, we started drifting apart five years ago. Its for the best. Maybe she may have met someone else, no, she said we would always be friends. Bugger it, I'm going to the pub.' He stayed until closing time.

Jack's head was nearly clear by the time he finished his second cup of coffee. 'Hate to think how much beer I drank yesterday, I know I spent all my money. I remember dinner was hamburger and chips, I can still taste the onion. I remember I had a couple of political arguments, nothing serious. Oh, that's right, that city slicker kept telling me what a great guy Muldoon had been. He didn't like it when I told him he was the father of our destruction. That other guy didn't appreciate me telling him that MMP stood for Mickey Mouse Politics. No harm in a bit of good-natured stirring. No, mostly talked football, life's like football, you win some, you lose some.'

The day was hot. It was that time of the year when the weather couldn't make up its mind whether it was still summer or threatening winter. Jack decided to get out in the garden, but his mind wasn't on it. He bumbled through the morning doing odd small jobs without much enthusiasm. By midday he had had enough.

'Only answer, open a brew. The sun's over the yardarm. A nice beer should just about bring me back to normal, or the land of the living, if that's normal. God I'm rambling again,' Jack said out loud.

'Hope no one can hear me. Mind you I've told the neighbours I talk to Sid.' Jack took a bottle of his homebrew out of the fridge and sat on the terrace. 'Can't beat Jack's Joyous Juice.'

After the beer, he ate a light lunch. All the time his brain was in overdrive thinking about his future. Now completely alone, the end of their marriage, the good times, then losing his job.

'Too expensive to keep on,' they said. As a middle management man, he could understand that. Get him out, save money by putting me off, then go on a major TV publicity campaign, spend money on new computers and renovate the offices.' Jack brooded.

'Thirty years with the same company. From labouring to factory manager, worker to boss.' The company had gone from a family business, then been gobbled up by a major corporation, then sold off.

'Yes, departmentalized, divisionalised, corporatize then privatized. Then the fateful day, "thanks for your devoted service, goodbye, there's six week's pay, sorry no redundancy, we are broke, we have to cut back," the big chief said. Yeah, and a week later him and his wife off to the States for six weeks, marketing and promotion, more like a holiday, and him swanning around in the latest BMW.'

'No money,' said Jack aloud. 'Too much going in the back pocket instead of the business.' Jack was getting agitated by this stage as the downsides of the past two years came back to him. 'Then the bloody inevitable. I think I'll go for a swim, it could be the last one.'

Jack's mind was miles away when Ma Johnson called out to him as he walked through the reserve towards the beach. 'Still swimming, Jack?'

'Yeah, could be the last one.' Jack replied as he walked on. A bit rude I suppose, Jack thought. He usually stopped and talked to the old lady. Today he wasn't in the mood. She was a good friend of Anne's, and he didn't feel like telling her that they had split. She would find out in time. Funny they all call her Ma when she had never married.

Jack went through his usual routine, slipped off his jandals, took off his straw hat, then dropped the towel over them, walked into the tide, splashing the water over his arms and chest. As the small waves reached his waist he dived under, then started to swim slowly out to sea his mind occupied with his recent problems.

Although not a strong swimmer, Jack normally swam around two hundred metres each day using a slow, but stylish freestyle action. As he swam he talked to himself.

'Damn government. If it wasn't for changing the retiring age, I'd still probably have a job. To think we used to carry guys for years after they turned sixty. Old Fred was useless, but no, the boss said, we can't put him off he's been with us too long, the union won't like it. A soon as that lot made retirement sixty-five and brought in the Contracts Act they soon got rid of Fred, and the other two pensioners we were carrying. Me, I never got the chance, down the road at fifty-five, nowadays no-one wants you if you are over fifty. Plus, I wasn't in a union anyway. Jack was boiling inside, his strokes got quicker.

'Retirement huh, those smart economists plan your retirement, start ten years before, learn a new skill each year. Bloody did that. Yeah - started at fifty, planned to finish with a new car, the whiteware all replaced, a few nice investments. There'll be none of that now, only a bike to ride and all the electrical appliances twenty years old and breaking down.'

'Oh, I did the skill thing. One year a writer's course, then the vegetable garden push, then the homebrew set up, did well there, then the learn-to-cook year, just as well, a better cook now. The last year was a failure, the repair-it-yourself course was a disaster. Always was, and still hopeless when it comes to fixing even the smallest jobs.' Jack laughed as he remembered the lecturer asking him if his favourite TV program was *Some Mothers Do Have Em*, 'Michael Crawford's got nothing on me.'

Jack was starting to power through the water, 'swimming well today,' he thought. 'Oh well, it's the last one.' His mind raced back to his previous thoughts.

'The last two years, yes, the last two years, pure damned survival. Doing everything on my own, the garden, housework, cooking, living on the dole, the whole hundred and forty odd dollars a week and the smart politicians say we're well off, I'd like to see some of them live off it. At least I own my own place.'

'They say we're dole bludgers. They forget I paid my taxes for forty years. I didn't ask to be put off work. Once they changed the rules it was easy for the bosses to get us old oldies out, then bring the kids in at cheap rates. As for that Grey Power lot, they were the old Muldoon supporters. Yeah, think big and we went broke.

They're all moaning now. At least they got a pension; the young ones today won't be so lucky.'

Jack started to feel tired. 'All this soapbox stuff. I've been through it a thousand times. Anyway I'm having my last swim. To Hell with the lot of them.'

As his stroke got slower Jack thought of Anne. 'A wonderful wife, great mother to our kids, and now a lovely gran to Sam. Pity to lose them, I'll miss Sam, only four, but as bright as a button. Maybe I should've tried harder to keep Anne. Oh, well, only fifty metres to go, have to get into sprint mode.'

Jack always thrashed out the last few metres. It was part of the daily ritual, to dream of the Olympic final, to swim the last part hard, hit the wall, turn, look at the scoreboard at the other end, see the light shining besides his name as the winner the time flashing, a new Olympic record, standing on the dais, the gold medal around his neck.

Jack turned to look at the scoreboard, instead he saw the shore five hundred metres away. He swallowed salt water. 'My God, I've swum out to sea.'

Like a smack in the face, he realized he hadn't swum out his usual ten metres, then made a right angle turn to swim parallel to the beach. He had kept swimming. Panic set in as he took in another mouthful of seawater. Cramp grabbed his right leg followed by the realization he had swum twice as far as usual.

'No wonder I'm feeling exhausted. I'll never get back. I've never swum that far in my life. What the Hell was I thinking of.'

Jack turned on his back, his mind again racing, not thinking of the past but of the job ahead of him. He could make out Ma Johnson standing on her terrace, a small blot from here. 'She won't see me, she's nearly blind. I'm on my own. I've got to make it,'

He lay on his back for several minutes, slowly regaining his strength, motivating himself for the task ahead. He thought of his grandson, Sam. The screeching of a seagull overhead aroused Jack from his thoughts. There was Sid flying tight circles above him.

'God he's looking at me again. Okay, okay, I'll get back. You're just worried about tomorrow's breakfast.'

Jack turned over and forced his tired arms and legs to push him towards the shore. 'Thankfully the tide's going in and there's no big waves.' It was a long slow swim. Jack had to keep rolling over on to his back to rest and regain strength. Sid was always there, when he stopped too long the bird would start screeching and head towards the shore.

'That bird thinks I'm stupid. I know where the shore is.' Jack said to nobody. The cramps down his right leg worried him, he had suffered from these for the past year. Several times they gripped his foot, calf and thigh at the same time causing him to yell in agony. Twice he went under while trying to manipulate the offending muscle. Usually, the cramps occurred when he was resting on his back, by rolling over and swimming they eased off.

As Jack got closer to shore, he kept trying to stand on the bottom. Frustration at not touching sand caused Jack to swear and curse Anne, the government, his old bosses, anything that came to mind.

Finally, his feet touched solid ground. Totally exhausted he walked up the beach. He felt stupid blaming everyone else for his own shortcomings and problems. Jack looked upwards for Sid. He wasn't there, he had disappeared. He looked down at his gear, slowly dried himself with the towel, turning aside the urge to lay down and rest before the walk up the hill. Jack realized once he lay down, he would be there a long time.

Ma Johnson was in her usual place as Jack labouriously climbed the path. 'Thought you were swimming to Great Barrier – I nearly called out the coastguard. You okay?'

'Yes, Ma, just missed the crossroads on the way out. Thought I'd have a good one seeing it was my last swim for the season. See you later, time I got home to cook tea.' Jack replied.

'I thought it was going to be your last swim forever. I was real worried you weren't going to make it back. You took ages.'

Jack smiled. She certainly didn't miss much. He was shivering when he got home. He turned on the shower, gradually building up the heat as his body became attuned to it, staying under the shower until the hot water supply ran out. It took two towels and a lot of hard rubbing to finally dry him off and return the feeling to his body. He put on warm clothing and opened a brew. After only one glass and before it was even dark, he went to bed.

Nightmares wracked Jack all night. He woke sweating profusely as he battled huge seas, or as he touched the bottom only to find he was under the water. He was swimming like crazy to evade the sharks, or looking up to a hundred seagulls dive-bombing his head, or the shore disappearing as he swam towards it.

At daylight Jack woke, his heart beating rapidly. 'My God the house is on fire.' He leaped out of bed and grabbed his clothes. Slowly he sat back on the edge of the bed. He pulled back the curtain to see a magnificent red sunrise. 'Slow down man,' he said quietly as he climbed back into bed and drifted off to sleep.

Later Jack woke. Bells were ringing. Birds were screeching. Jack shook the cobwebs out of his brain, he realized the phone was ringing and Sid was doing his late breakfast act outside.

Jack picked up the phone. 'Hello Granddad, how are you? I thought you had gone. How's Sid?' It was Sam.

I nearly was gone, thought Jack. 'No, I'm here, Sam. I'm okay. I had my last swim for the season yesterday. Sid's outside yelling for his breakfast, I better go and feed him. See you later, Sam.'

We didnt do too bad for two kids who left school at fifteen with no trade or qualifications.

Lynn and Norm, 24/10/2022

ready for the last voyage

www.ingramcontent.com/pod-product-compliance
Lightning Source LLC
Chambersburg PA
CBHW051627120626
46551CB00014B/1968